THE BOOK OF
JOB

Introduction and Commentary

by

ANTHONY AND MIRIAM HANSON

SCM PRESS LTD
BLOOMSBURY STREET LONDON

334 00796 8

First published 1953
by SCM Press Ltd
56 Bloomsbury Street London WC1
Second impression 1958
Third impression 1962
Fourth impression 1970
Fifth impression 1972
Sixth impression 1976

© *SCM Press Ltd 1953*

Printed in Great Britain by
Fletcher & Son Ltd, Norwich

TORCH BIBLE
COMMENTARIES

CONTENTS

I

THE FIRST CYCLE OF SPEECHES
Chapters 3-11

II

THE SECOND CYCLE OF SPEECHES
Chapters 12-20

5

III

THE THIRD CYCLE OF SPEECHES
Chapters 21-31

IV

SECOND INTERPOLATION: ELIHU'S SPEECH

V

GOD'S APPEARANCE AND JOB'S SUBMISSION
Chapters 38-42.6

EPILOGUE

INTRODUCTION

Section 1

THE STRUCTURE OF THE BOOK OF JOB

By far the greater part of the Book of Job is written in poetry. Even when we read the Book in our Authorized Version, where it is not printed in verse form, we can feel the poetry breaking through. But this poetic portion is introduced by a prose narrative, often called the Prologue (chapters 1 and 2), and is followed by a short prose Epilogue (chapter 42.7 to end). This division between the prose Prologue and Epilogue on the one hand and, on the other, the long poem which comes between, constitutes one of the main problems of the book, for the difference does not consist only in the form in which these sections are written.

When we compare the Prologue and Epilogue with the rest of the book, we find that not only does the form differ, but there are great differences in the contents and style. The Prologue and Epilogue give us a picture of an ideal patriarch, a pious man who has been rewarded for his piety by worldly prosperity. At the suggestion of the Satan, or Accusing Angel, Job is by God's decree deprived of all his possessions and even of his family, as a test of his fidelity to God. Job survives this test admirably, accepting both good and evil fortune patiently at God's hand. Then, in the Epilogue, he is restored to his former estate, his attitude towards God commended and his friends rebuked for the unworthy way in which they attempted to console him in the time of his misfortune. But in the poetical part a very different Job is presented to us. Instead of the pious patriarch of the Prologue

7

and Epilogue, we find an indignant sufferer, who violently protests against the treatment which he has received at God's hands, and alternates passionate prayers to God that He should let him alone to die with confident assertions of his own innocence and God's injustice. Even more mysterious is the fact that some at least of the arguments of the three friends, far from being repudiated by God, are actually used by God Himself, when He finally appears in response to Job's angry appeals (chapters 38-41). Add finally that in the poem, as opposed to the prose Prologue-Epilogue, no notice whatever is taken of the Satan's scheme for testing Job's sincerity, and that this ready-made explanation of all Job's suffering is simply ignored, and you will see that there is no small problem raised at the outset by the very structure of the book itself.

It is only within the last century that this problem has been much understood. Before that the belief in the verbal inspiration and infallibility of the Bible, which was accepted by almost all Christians, prevented anyone from really admitting that there was a problem at all. The pious side of Job's character, as presented in the Prologue and Epilogue, was emphasized, and his daring and indeed shocking accusations against God in the poem were either ignored or explained away. (As we shall see, there is some evidence that even before the completion of the book as we now have it, pious scribes among the Jews themselves made some efforts to tone down Job's accusations.) But with the rise of biblical criticism in the last century, and the consequent abandonment by nearly all Christian scholars of the theory of verbal inspiration, it became possible to look at the book in a new light, and at once the disparity between the prose and the verse parts of the book stood out. Various explanations have been put forward; the most recent writers seem to favour the drastic view that the Prologue and Epilogue were actually written by someone different from the author of the poem, and that this prose-writer added his contribution afterwards in the hope of giving a more respectable appearance to the work as a whole. But so extreme a theory is not necessary, and indeed leaves many questions unanswered. The best line of approach to the problem lies in the realization that the story of Job is neither a piece of literal history nor a story made up by the author of the Book of Job to suit his purpose; it is an old legend which runs back into the earliest period of the history of the Jews. We find a mention of Job in the Book of Ezekiel, which was written probably more than a hundred years before the Book of Job itself. In Ezekiel 14.14 the prophet associates Job with Noah and Daniel as examples of men of proverbial piety. Even more significant than this, scholars in recent years have actually found traces of a 'Babylonian Job', that is, a fragment of a Babylonian legend, which bears a strong resemblance to the Job story. The fragment dates only from the seventh century B.C., but the legend is probably much older. The fragment is part of a poem, in which a king (he is not called Job) begins by mourning his miserable estate; he claims he has been regular in his religious duties, reflects on the inscrutable will of the gods, and describes his malady. The poem ends with his restoration. He apparently admits he has sinned, but cannot discover what his sin was, and is most anxious to find out.

Another interesting parallel comes from Hindu legend. Here a righteous king called Harischandra is tempted by a supernatural being called a Rishi, who has made a wager with a fellow-Rishi that no man's righteousness is proof against temptation. Harischandra undergoes every form of trial in order to induce him to fail in his duty (the Hindu word is *dharma*, which means the duties belonging to that state of life into which it *has pleased* God to call us). But in every circumstance of ignominy and disaster Harischandra resolutely performs his *dharma*, so in the end his fortunes are restored and the wicked Rishi loses his wager. The parallel with the Job legend is very close indeed here, but it is expressed in terms of the Hindu conception of righteousness.

Now once we have realized that there was a legend of Job, we can begin to understand why there is this contrast between Prologue-Epilogue and the rest of the book. The author of the Book of Job has used the well-known legend of Job to form a setting for his poem. There were certain problems in connection with God's government of the world and the relation between God and man that he wanted to deal with in his poem, and he thought that the legend of Job would make a suitable context in which to set his discussion. The author of Job chose the legend because it gave him a man at the point at which he wanted him, but his treatment of his theme is so much more profound than the conventional piety of the legend that the contrast between his Job and the legendary Job is almost ironic. We can find a parallel in the Greek dramatist Euripides, who wrote at about 400 B.C. In several of his plays he takes a traditional story about the gods, but so treats it as to show its injustice and absurdity when judged by the more enlightened standards of his day. Not that the author of Job had any idea of ridiculing the Job legend. The resemblance lies in the fact that both poets have taken traditional material, and greatly altered it to suit their purposes.

This approach to the problem of the Prologue-Epilogue also goes far to explain the difference of style between the prose and the verse parts of the book. It is not likely that the author of the book had to incorporate an already written Prologue and Epilogue into his work; he probably wrote them both himself. But the conventions of the legend imposed a certain style upon him as long as he was writing about legendary events. Job in the legend was an ideal patriarch, and that meant that he had to offer sacrifice on altars he built himself to God as the patriarchs did in Genesis, and that when he was restored to prosperity that prosperity should be expressed in terms of twice as much worldly goods as before, seven sons and three daughters more beautiful than any other ladies in the land. It is very much as if a modern poet, wishing to write on the theme of the rise of the humble and the fall of the mighty, were to take the story of Cinderella as his setting. We would naturally expect the traditional fairy-story style, with the lovely, good-natured, ill-treated heroine, the wicked sisters and the handsome prince, and so on. It seems therefore quite beside the point to treat the details of the Prologue-Epilogue as if they were part of a novel, and described a character which the author was trying to make to come alive before us. For instance, one modern editor writes thus of 1.5, where Job is described as offering a sacrifice in case his children should have sinned unintentionally in their festivities: 'Job himself was not present at the festivities of his children . . . did not wish to impose his gravity on those whose years it did not suit. . . . What he feared in them was not any open excess . . . but a momentary turning away from God in the midst of social enjoyment, as if they felt this was better than religion.' Thus to moralize the events of the first chapter is to miss the point of them. It is part of the traditional setting, which the author adapted from his legendary material.

Though the climate changes sharply when we pass from chapter 2 to chapter 3, our author did not forget even in his poem that his subject was supposed to be living in the patriarchal age. It is remarkable that there is no reference whatever to Israel, or anything to do with Israel's history, throughout the book. Job is usually classed with books like Proverbs and Ecclesiastes as Wisdom literature, and this is one of the characteristics of such writings. Similarly Job himself and all his friends are represented as being independent chiefs. The description of Job in his former prosperity in chapters 29 to 31 is a picture of a wealthy and powerful oriental chieftain, owning lands and flocks and meting out justice to his dependents. This lack of clear connection with the history of the Old Testament is no doubt why the Book of Job has so often been treated as a fine piece of work, but one which is quite off the main track of development of the Old Testament, a sort of theological by-way that led nowhere. Reason is shown in the next section for believing that the contrary is true, and that the Book of Job actually is an important link between the Old Testament and the New. But we can see why it was necessary for the author of the book to maintain his patriarchal setting throughout. He was treating of problems which he believed to be universal, and which did not essentially depend on the special relationship which existed between God and Israel. Of course, if he had not begun with the knowledge of God which Israel had acquired through the centuries, he could never have written what he did; but his problems were universal problems, and for such a discussion some sort of a universal setting, freed from the particular circumstances of Israel's history, was necessary.

The legend of Job is not the only traditional material which our author uses; we find scattered throughout the book reference to primitive myths and folk-lore which were part of the original religious heritage of the Semitic peoples before the Jews began to be marked off by their special understanding of God's nature and purposes. Thus in 9.13 we find a reference to Rahab, or Tiamat, the original chaos-monster, whom God was believed to have conquered when He formed the world (the reference is obscured in the A.V.; see the Commentary in that place). Similarly in 26.13 we have another reference to God's victory over the primeval monster. In 38.31 God refers to His mighty act in chaining the giant Orion in the sky, and in 3.8 reference seems to be made to the snake that swallows the sun in an eclipse (once more the A.V. is obscure; see note there). In 18.13-14 we have the names or at least the titles of two demons held in awe by the Hebrews. This does not at all imply that our author necessarily believed in the literal truth of all these legends and myths, any more than Shakespeare believed in the existence of Oberon and Titania. He used them as materials in his poem. The question of whether they were literally true or not probably never occurred to him.

So far we have only looked at one great feature of the structure of the Book of Job, the difference between the Prologue-Epilogue and the rest of the book, and its significance; but one can see other minor divisions also. If you look at the contents at the beginning of this Commentary, you will see that the poem has been divided into five main sections. The first three of these are called 'Cycles of Speeches' because in each one we have first a speech by Job, then a speech by each of the three friends. But Job always replies to each friend after that friend has spoken, so Job speaks three times for each time that any one friend speaks. This arrangement is not maintained in the third cycle, which has not come down to us entire. Though for the sake of clarity each Cycle of Speeches has been marked off from the others in the Contents and Commentary, there is no original line of division between the cycles in this poem. For example, chapters 12 and 13 might just as well be Job's final reply to the first cycle as his beginning the second. These Cycles of Speeches conclude with chapters 29 to 31, in which Job, having apparently silenced his friends, makes his last great challenge to God to appear. Then comes the fourth section, the speech of Elihu. But there are very strong reasons for believing that these chapters, 32 to 37, were not part of the original work. Reasons for thinking they were added afterwards by some later writer are given in the Commentary at chapter 32. So, if we are to follow the original plan of the work its sequence is as follows: after Job has challenged God to appear (chap. 31) God does appear (chap. 38) and answers Job. This is the fifth section; it contains both God's appearance to Job and Job's submission to God.

If you look at the Contents again, you will see that, besides Elihu's speech in chapters 32 to 37, described in the Contents as the Second Interpolation, there are two other Interpolations. The first of these is chapter 28, written in praise of Wisdom. This too is probably not by the author of Job, but was inserted later by some other hand (for reasons for this view see the Commentary). The Third Interpolation is chapter 40.15 to 41 end, and contains a description of two great creatures, probably the hippopotamus and crocodile. Again see the Commentary at this point for the reasons which make most scholars believe this to be a later addition. Of these three interpolations, only the Elihu chapters form a really serious interruption to the course of the argument; but we must try and imagine them as absent if we want to grasp the main outline of the Book of Job, as it left the hands of its author.

Section 2

WHAT IS THE BOOK OF JOB ABOUT?

Usually to such a question there is a clear traditional answer on which the majority of readers can readily agree. When we ask this question about the Book of Job, however, we come straight to the problem on whose solution depends the value of the book for us, and its importance in the Bible.

The legend of Job as it is contained in the Prologue-Epilogue has been described above. In the poem, Job's first speeches are passionate cries of woe and protest that these things should have come on him. After each speech, one friend after another takes up the challenge of Job's words, and attempts to 'speak to his condition'. Job's words grow in vehemence and in depth and he passes from his immediate problem to the whole question of the nature of God and of righteousness. He feels God Himself is hidden from him, and he seeks above all an encounter with the God who blessed him of old. The friends in reply argue persistently that suffering is the wages of sin. Job is suffering, therefore he must have sinned, yes, he *has* sinned grossly, and must repent and wait for God's good pleasure. If he does this, why of course God will restore to him his former prosperity, for though He is inscrutable in glory and majesty His rewards to the good are as sure as His punishment of the wicked. Job ruthlessly demonstrates the opposite point—that God does *not* punish the wicked. They flourish, and the good are often social outcasts. In a final long and beautiful speech, he makes his declaration of integrity. Thereupon (if we disregard the Elihu speeches) God appears, and answers Job by a display of majesty and inscrutable power, and shows how utterly futile it is for man to stand before God and assert his own righteousness. He has none to assert, when faced with that glory. Job submits to this vision and repents. The Epilogue completes the tale with his restitution to double his former wealth and happiness.

There are many subjects touched on in greater or less detail. Disinterested obedience to God under testing, innocent suffering, social oppression, religious experience and pious duty, a man's relation to God and the nature of that God—where in all this can we find the key that lets the book be seen as a unified whole? Is it indeed possible to find one, or must such an attempt be abandoned and the Book of Job seen as a patchwork, as some editors suggest?

Of the possible lines of approach, two perhaps stand out as the main interpretations, and they might be called 'The Patience of a Good Man under Testing', and 'The Problem of Innocent Suffering'. We will look at them in turn.

The Patience of a Good Man under Testing

It will be remembered that the Prologue sets the scene and suggests that Satan received permission to tempt Job to prove his lack of faithfulness, and that in the Epilogue God commends Job for his obedience in spite of the severe trial. The New Testament writers refer only once to Job by name. This reference is in the Epistle of James, where the writer uses it as an outstanding example of patience. Usually where Job is treated in the early literature of the Church, this theme of patient bearing under the testing of God is seen as its message. Early tradition takes its cue from James' reference, and 'the patience of Job' has passed into proverb. But while in the prose narrative Job certainly is patient, it is a very different character who bursts forth into passionate pleas against God, who bemoans his own birth and cries for justification. This second Job is as impatient under affliction as King Lear himself. The impression early exegesis of Job gives is that the readers knew the prose parts well, and left the great poem undigested, except for a few star passages where they thought they could detect a belief in the resurrection of the body. For centuries Job was the patient sufferer, and prophet of the resurrection.

The Problem of Innocent Suffering

When nineteenth-century scholars began, with their greater critical equipment, to look into the Book of Job, they generally proclaimed its main theme to be, not the testing of Job, but the problem of the suffering of an innocent man. Of course, this is one of the most prominent themes in the book, and it is amazing how long it was left in the background. Here is a man, obviously righteous, and yet subjected to all manner of distresses. How can we explain his experience? Traditional answers, as represented by the friends, just will not do, for they are not true to our experience. The good do often suffer, and the evil do flourish. In the view of these scholars of the nineteenth century we are left at the end of the Book of Job, not with a patient sufferer, but with a greatly deepened view of the problem of suffering in general. Job's experience teaches that we must rest in faith in an inscrutable God, whose ways are far past our understanding, and we must not seek to explain or confine His acts to the limits of our knowledge. Several commentators of this time, however, thought that the author of the Book of Job intended counselling resignation, and nothing more. In this case, the view of the writer of the Book of Job is to be found in the mouth of the three friends.

But although the problem of innocent suffering has been claimed as the main theme of Job, almost all commentators would admit this emphasis does not account for everything in the book. In fact, it leaves us with a very real difficulty. If this is the main and supreme argument and if the answer to the cry of an innocent man in his agony is a vision of overwhelming majesty and inscrutable providence, then not only do the friends forestall God's reply and get rebuked for their pains, but the reply itself leaves us very much where we were. After a poem which clearly shows itself to be the vision and insight of a great and daring mind, we are brought down at the end to the level of the friends' understanding of the matter, which is nowhere so profound as Job's. We have the feeling of reaching darkness rather than light. A mystery has been probed, little help given, and the unconvincing conclusion only deepens the mystery. Was this really all the author of Job was trying to convey by his poem? Or is his central message to be found in another emphasis, set against this background of the agony of a man's sufferings?

Man's Righteousness Before God

We have already seen that the author made use of traditional material as the framework of his poem. The severe trials of Job were known in legend long before our author wrote. It seems most probable that he selected this legend because it gave him a man, a good and pious man, so placed that the most fundamental questions were bound to agonize his heart. Job's severe afflictions—loss of worldly property, bereavement, suffering of body and the absence of sympathetic understanding on the part of wife and friends—these colour the first part of his speeches. But very soon we come to the fundamental questions which torment him: how can a man be just before God? How can I stand before God? Will He not come and reveal Himself and let me justify myself to Him? Let me show Him my integrity of purpose and my good deeds. What sort of a God is this who even hides Himself from me now? These are questions which complacent piety, when it is secure in material comfort, can never frame but which inevitably spring to the lips of the sufferer. Doubts and questionings arise when the stable, invariable order of events is shattered by some cataclysm, and the hand of God is in those doubts, even if not quite in the way pictured in the old legend of Job. George Macdonald, writing on Job, remarks: 'To deny the existence of God may involve less unbelief than the smallest yielding to doubt of His goodness. I say yielding, for a man may be haunted with doubts and only grow thereby in faith. Doubts are the messengers of the Living One to the honest. . . . Doubt must precede every deeper assurance, for uncertainties are what we first see when we look into a region hitherto unknown, unexplored, unannexed. . . .' Job's sufferings bring him to the threshold of this experience.

Job's passionate pleading of his own righteousness, his calling upon God to witness against Himself, lead him on to an encounter with the Living God, which is the only answer to that particular question. The encounter is no answer to the question, 'Why do the righteous suffer?' But the appearance of God, and Job's humiliation before Him is the only answer to the plea, 'Let me meet God and justify myself to Him'. At the moment of his calling (if, as suggested above, the Elihu speeches are set aside as a later interpolation) God answers him by the only way known to the deepest thought of the O.T. —direct revelation. The effect on Job is not what he expected, and he finds what everyone who has ever met the Living God experiences. To quote George Macdonald further: 'Seeing God, Job forgets all he wanted to say, all he thought he would say if he could but see Him. Job had his desire: he saw the face of God and abhorred himself in dust and ashes. He sought justification, he found self-abhorrence.' Unlike that young man in the gospels who came to our Lord similarly armed with a protestation of good conduct, Job capitulates at once. He has no wealth, no security to hide in from the Living God.

Job's questions, however, plainly shocked not only the friends in the poem, but copyists and scribes too. The friends pour out on him all that traditional piety can say, repeating again and again the very theory of God's actions that seems exploded once and for all by Job's experience. Good for the good, and bad for the bad. Those who receive evil must be evil. Do good and you cannot fail of your material reward, and so on. This notion of piety is very much the upright, un-pitying attitude of the ideal Jew of Psalm 1, without compassion and complacent in his superior position. Not so long ago one heard echoes of this type of piety in such remarks as ' But they are such good people! Why should *their* house be bombed?'

Surely here the author of the Book of Job had a message for his own people, those upright, self-righteous folk, whose later day sins came to fruit in our Lord's day and blinded them to His nature and authority. Behind the figure of the one sufferer and his companions stands a whole people, expecting favoured treatment because of their virtues, indignant with God because of their sufferings, and losing their humility. They needed to learn afresh what the greatest of them throughout their history always knew, that justification only comes by faith in God, and not by self-vindication.

It is worth while recalling here another Old Testament book which had a message for the same people, directed against a sin very much akin to that of Job. The author of the Book of Jonah deals hardly with his countrymen's unwillingness to allow themselves to be the messengers of God's grace to all. They knew themselves chosen of God and knew enough of His grace to resent outsiders sharing in it. It is significant that where the doctrine of the Book of Job (and its New Testament enlargement in Romans) is well understood—i.e. that it is only by faith that justification can come—the missionary calling preached by Jonah is at once felt in its full compelling power. The Jewish people needed to absorb the message of the Book of Job, and the related theme of Jonah, for both are splendidly prophetic in their own way of the coming of our Lord.

If the standing of a man before God is indeed the main theme of the Book of Job, what are we to make of the problem which occasions the whole discussion, the suffering of a righteous man? To this problem the book offers no answer. The friends' attempts are certainly not profound enough to come to grips with it, and God's reply gives no single word to Job that can illumine this mystery. In fact only one other place in the Old Testament does offer an answer which is at all satisfying. When we compare the Suffering Servant passages in Isaiah 40-55 with Job, it is plain at once that they contain a far more profound idea of the nature of innocent suffering. In Isaiah 53 the Servant is shown willingly submitting to suffering all things for the sake of his brethren. He suffers that they may be spared. The passage brings to mind our Lord's words about the highest form of love a man can show, to lay down his life for his friends. But this depth of love, that suffers for its loved ones, is only an image and foretaste of the love that can accept even the cruellest suffering for the sake of those who are its enemies. Our Lord's divinity was never plainer than in His laying down His life ' while we were yet sinners ', and no sufferer has been more sinless than He. Such a conception of suffering goes as far beyond the natural love of which many are capable as our Lord is beyond us. We know from Him that wherever there is suffering, He suffers with the sufferer. But for an approach to the problem of innocent suffering that can be of comfort and solace to the Christian in trouble, it is not wise to look to the Book of Job, where it is not the paramount problem and receives no full answer.

On the other hand, no account of the history of the dealings of God with men, and of the way of faith, not works, as the approach to Him is complete without full justice being done to this book. The author shows the deepest understanding of the fundamental requirements of the Jewish law. He makes Job claim a clear record on all points of which a book such as Deuteronomy insists. His claim to have dealt justly and mercifully is emphasized. He goes further, and reaches a point of insight not often found in the Old Testament, and only given its true place in the Sermon on the Mount. Job recognizes the inward claims of the law. For example, that it is no use claiming to be free from the sin of adultery, even though one may be pure in deed, if there is lust in one's heart. In his last long plea to God, he dwells on this theme of the purity of his intentions. But even in this assertion of purity, there are no grounds for any claim on God. Even the pure heart cannot justify a man, and while God, appearing in glory and majesty, accepts Job and redeems him (this surely is the meaning of the ' fairy-tale ' ending) it is the contrite, broken-hearted Job who receives this salvation. The Job to whom God reveals Himself in glory could make Psalm 51 his prayer and rejoice in his weakness.

The Christian has been given just what Job asked for in chapter 13—a God who has removed His awe and revealed His ways. But the Christian is still unable to make out a case for his own righteousness in the way Job expected, as *he* is overwhelmed with the glory shown, not in the whirlwind, but on the Cross. The voice on the Damascus Road had the same effect on Paul as the vision of God's majesty on Job. Both the Old Testament poet's character and Saul of Tarsus cease their efforts after self-justification and salvation by works, and rest in faith.

Section 3

THE BOOK OF JOB AND THE NEW TESTAMENT

Few books in the Old Testament seem at first sight to have less connection with the N.T. than the Book of Job. Direct quotations are almost non-existent. There are a few in the Pauline epistles, one apparently in Matthew's Gospel, and perhaps two in Luke's writings. Apart from this, there are a number of places where Job appears to be echoed rather than quoted. If one were to judge simply by the statistics of quotations, one would say that the N.T. writers did not understand the Book of Job and were not interested in it.

To some extent this is true: certainly the N.T. writers do not show any evidence of a deep understanding of the Book. They did not look on the Book of Job as they looked, for example, on the Book of Isaiah or the Psalms, as a book filled with prophecies of the coming of the Messiah. But just because the central theme of the Book of Job is so closely related to the central theme of the N.T., there are in fact several remarkable points of correspondence between it and the Book of Job. It is in itself a significant fact that there are almost as many echoes and quotations from Job in Paul's letters as in the rest of the N.T. put together; and it is even more significant that seven such echoes occur in the Epistle to the Romans alone. Paul had no thought of expounding the Book of Job, but what he was trying to say himself was in some respects so similar to the message of Job that the words of the Book of Job come naturally to Paul's lips. We can sum up these resemblances under the two headings: 'God's Unpredictability', and 'God's Righteousness'.

God's Unpredictability

God's unpredictability is a prominent theme in Job. The friends refer to it just as much as Job does, only the friends interpret it in a beneficent sense, while Job tends to look on

God as unpredictable in a sinister way. But Paul in his own context emphasizes the unpredictability of God also; writing his first letter to the Corinthians, he writes of what he, with a startling paradox calls 'the foolishness of God' and the 'weakness of God'. He means the Cross, that unpredictable action of God whereby He shocked both Jews and Gentiles. But, says Paul, that very Christ crucified is, to those who believe, 'the power of God and the wisdom of God' (I Cor. 1.24). This may be an echo of Daniel 2.20-21, but it may just as well be an echo of Job 12.16. WITH HIM IS STRENGTH AND WISDOM, and Job goes on THE DECEIVED AND THE DECEIVER ARE HIS. Job also is emphasizing that you cannot predict God's actions, though he never guessed that God's unpredictability would one day take the form of the Cross. Since the friends also agree on God's unpredictability, it is not surprising that another Pauline echo comes from the speech of Eliphaz: HE TAKETH THE WISE IN THEIR OWN CRAFTINESS (Job 5.13) is quoted by Paul in 1 Cor. 3.19. Paul quotes, again no doubt with the Cross in mind, in order to show that: 'The wisdom of this world is foolishness with God,' and he draws the moral: 'Therefore let no man glory in men.' There is another Pauline passage where he seems to echo two other passages from Job, i.e., Romans 11.33. 'How unsearchable are his (God's) judgements, and his ways past finding out!' Once more the Cross is in the background: Paul is marvelling at God's method of justifying men through the life and death and resurrection of Jesus Christ. He seems to be echoing Job 5.9 and 11.7, both passages from the friends' speeches. But of course the friends are arguing in favour of the traditional explanation of God's behaviour, which, they say, should not be challenged, while Paul is expounding the great new act of God in Christ.

There is a little group of passages in the Gospels where Job seems to be echoed. One occurs in the Song of the Virgin Mary in Luke 1.52, 'He hath put down the mighty from their seats, and exalted them of low degree'. This seems to be an echo of Job 5.11 and 12.19, one from Eliphaz's speech and one from Job's. Again Job's final confession of helplessness

in 42.2, I KNOW THAT THOU CANST DO EVERYTHING seems to
find its echo in two sentences of our Lord's. The first is
Matthew 19.26, where He is speaking of the rich entering the
Kingdom of God. The second is Mark 14.36, where our
Lord in His agony in the garden says: 'Abba, Father, all
things are possible unto thee.' We can say of these what we
said of the Pauline passages, that they express the same truth
about God as is expressed in Job, but are written when that
truth has been revealed in a far more marvellous and un-
expected way than the author of Job ever guessed. Job accepting the revelation of God in the whirlwind, and our Lord
accepting the Cross as the will of the Father, are in the same
succession.

God's Righteousness

The unpredictability of God is only one theme in Job. But
the righteousness of God might be called the central theme of
the Book, and it is here that the correspondence with Paul's
thought is most significant. This correspondence is not
marked here so much by actual quotation as by similarity of
sentiment, or by passages in Job which seem to stand in need
of passages from Paul's writings to complete them. But there
is one actual quotation; in Philippians 1.19, Paul, writing from
prison, speaks of the various hindrances to the preaching of
the Gospel which have occurred. But, he says, the Gospel
is, somehow or other, preached; and he adds: 'I know that
this shall turn to my salvation.' This is actually a quotation
from Job 13.16, though the quotation is obscured through the
faulty translation of the A.V. in Job: HE ALSO SHALL BE MY
SALVATION. It should be: 'This shall be my salvation'; the
Greek of Job 13.16, which was the language in which Paul
read the book, and the Greek of Philippians 1.19, are identical.
The contrast is as significant as the resemblance. What Job
hopes will be his salvation is his own integrity. Paul repudi-
ates any such idea (See Phil. 3.9); what Paul looks for as his
salvation is simply that the Gospel of the free grace of God
should be preached. But the Job who in chapter 13 feels such

confidence in his own integrity is not the Job of the end of
the book. What Job learns at the end is that his own righteousness cannot stand before God, that God is more righteous than
man. So the message of the Book of Job points to the same
conclusion as Paul arrives at, that in the light of God's
righteousness man's righteousness disappears.

The same significant contrast between Job's self-confident
righteousness and the righteousness of God as revealed in
Jesus Christ is brought out by a comparison of Job 29.15
with Romans 2.19. In chapter 29 Job is describing his former
condition, wherein he was able to display all his virtues of
generosity and he says: I WAS EYES TO THE BLIND. Paul in
Romans 2 is describing the condition of the self-righteous
Jew, who looks down on the heathen in his blindness; Paul
says of him 'And thou art confident that thou thyself are a
guide of the blind, a light of them which are in darkness.'
Both the author of Job and Paul came to the realization that
this sort of self-righteousness was not enough. This is why
chapter 31 of Job brings us so near to the N.T.; we have
pointed out in the Commentary on that chapter how remarkable are the parallels with the Gospels and especially with the
Sermon on the Mount. Job, in delineating the character which
he bore in the days of his prosperity, has described a standard
of morality which approaches in many ways that which our
Lord demands in His teaching. Mere outward conformity is
not enough for Job; he realizes that it is the inward assent of
the heart that really matters, and that it is the inward sin in the
intention that is really culpable. And yet, in the eyes of the
author of Job, even this lofty standard of morality was not
enough. What man can offer to God, in the last analysis, is
not his own integrity, no matter how spiritually conceived, but
a broken heart, an admission of sin such as Job makes in the
end.

It is because the author of Job realized that man must stand
before God as a sinner who has no resource left in himself,
that in several places we feel as we read Job's speech that Job
is just about to stumble on the discovery that God is a God

of grace and love. Again and again, as Job expresses his relation to God in legal terms, we almost expect to hear the voice of Paul telling us that God's righteousness in Christ has transcended the Law. This is especially so in chapter 9 where Job imagines himself as appearing before God in a court of law. He protests in verses 11 onwards that he has no hope of victory in such a suit; his plea would be unheard and finally in verse 15 he suggests that his only hope would be in throwing himself on the mercy of his judge. I WOULD MAKE SUPPLICATION TO MY JUDGE; instead of JUDGE we ought to read 'adversary at law'. The remarkable thing is that this is precisely what Paul in Romans argues that we must do: 'O wretched man that I am! who shall deliver me from the body of this death? I thank God through Jesus Christ our Lord' (Romans 7.24 to 25). By the end of the Book, Job had perhaps reached the point of saying: 'O wretched man that I am!': that is the measure of the profundity of our author's thought. What he could not foresee was the amazing mercy of God, the fact that Job's adversary should prove to be his saviour. He could not foresee the Cross and therefore could not, like Paul, understand that when we do throw ourselves on the mercy of our adversary we find that we are in the hands of a loving God. Just the same point arises in 9.33, where Job longs for a DAYSMAN or 'arbiter' between himself and God. Christian commentators have rejoiced to see here a prophecy of the atonement of Christ as the daysman between God and man. But in fact Christ when He came was not at all the sort of arbiter which Job imagined. He came not to effect a compromise between two parties, far less to vindicate the righteous unjustly treated by God, as Job suggests. He came to save, and in His saving to condemn. He came to conclude all under sin, that all might be saved.

We might trace here an interesting parallel between Job's argument against God and the way it is answered on the one hand, and Paul's account of God's use of the Law on the other. The whole force of Job's plea against God lies in the assumption that God, by inflicting these sufferings upon him, shows that He holds Job guilty—which, declares Job, is unjust. But when God appears, Job realizes that God entirely transcends any such account of His actions. In the same way, Paul declares that God has in Jesus Christ transcended the Law. The Law was in its own time necessary; and Paul calls it holy, and ordained by God. But he has no doubt that God has now shown a better way and dispensed with the old one. The friends' description of God's government of the world was in its own time a necessary step forward in man's knowledge of God. It did at least provide a morally acceptable explanation of life. But by the time the Book of Job was written it had outgrown its use, and our author came forward to witness that it had been transcended. In each case we find a venerable conception, not without divine sanction in its day, transcended and superseded by a deeper apprehension of God.

If we want, then, to sum up the point wherein the Book of Job is most closely connected with the N.T., we can say that it is in the apprehension that even man's best righteousness affords no grounds on which he can approach God. In the light of this, 40.8 becomes extremely significant. God speaks to Job:

WILT THOU ALSO DISANNUL MY JUDGEMENT? WILT THOU CONDEMN ME, THAT THOU MAYEST BE RIGHTEOUS?

This is more than just silencing the man who presumes to criticize God. It is the repudiation of the idea that man can be righteous before God; it is the answer to Job's plea for a just judgement and it is as near to a conclusion to the argument as we get in the Book of Job. Man cannot plead his own righteousness before God. He can only bow before God's righteousness. How that righteousness is manifested we do not know, but man can, and must, trust God. This brings us to the very brink of the N.T. We are ready for the declaration of the free grace of God, the righteousness which is Jesus Christ.

The Place of the Book of Job in the Bible

Job often appears in stained glass windows pointing to our Lord and bearing a scroll with the words: I KNOW. THAT MY REDEEMER LIVETH. This would convey that the main significance of the Book of Job in the Bible is that it foreshadowed the Resurrection of Christ, or the resurrection of the body. This is very far from being the case: though the author of Job does in one or two places distantly contemplate the possibility of some sort of life beyond the grave, he puts no confidence in the possibility. The texts usually cited in support of this belief prove to have a different meaning. If we want a book in the O.T. that contains a belief in a future life, we can turn to the Book of Daniel. Scholars of the nineteenth century destroyed this misconception by the invaluable work which they did on the text and literary background of the Book of Job. They tended to substitute for the picture of the Prophet of the Resurrection another picture, the figure of the Innocent Sufferer. They saw the Book as mainly significant in the Bible because it brings into the light and courageously discusses the agonizing question of the suffering of the innocent.

If our conclusions in Section 2 about the theme of the Book are right, even this estimate of the Book's place in the Bible is not really adequate. The problem of innocent suffering is only the point where our author chooses that the argument shall begin. One hundred years before Job was written, the Second Isaiah had brought that problem before his people, and had given his own solution, in a way that could never be forgotten, and that was not to be surpassed for more than five hundred years. It is because Job feels that he is being unjustly punished that he so insistently pleads his own integrity and so urgently calls on God to justify him. Moreover, this problem does receive a solution. God when He appears contributes nothing to the discussion of innocent suffering, but He does show what the righteousness of man is worth, and what the righteousness of God implies. To quote a recent article on the Book of Job: 'There are two main lines of thought in the

O.T. concerning the achievement by man of reconciliation with God. One puts its trust in sacrifice and cultural and ritual correctness. The other (represented by Amos, Hosea, Isaiah, etc.) calls for the obedient humble mind . . . and the upright character. . . . The author of the Book of Job, alone among the O.T. writers, rejects both. . . . He proclaims quite clearly that the obedient heart . . . and the upright character (all of which Job had) do not avail to win righteousness with God.'

So the Book of Job occupies a most important position in the Bible. The author on one vitally important theme saw farther than anyone else in the O.T., and is entitled to rank with Hosea and the Second Isaiah as one whose insight into the ways of God makes him seem more like one who lived under the Christian dispensation. He poses a question which only the N.T. can answer: since the righteousness of man cannot stand before God, how is the righteousness of God manifested? St. Paul, above all other writers of the N.T., gives the best commentary on Job, and the coincidences between his writings and the Book of Job are all the more impressive for being not entirely intentional. The Book of Job does indeed foreshadow an all-important element in the New Testament—not the resurrection of the body, not even the vicarious suffering of the Man of Sorrows, but justification by faith in the Messiah who is the incarnate expression of the love of God.

Section 4

DATE, STYLE, TEXT, EDITIONS

Date and Authorship

There is probably no complete book in the O.T. which is
more difficult to date exactly than Job. On the other hand,
there is probably no book whose date of writing is less significant for the message as a whole. The traditional view was
that it was written in the patriarchal age, as the scene was
obviously set in that period by its author. Hence the date
1520 B.C. assigned in the A.V. So Moses was an obvious
choice for authorship. Scientific study of its vocabulary, however, makes it clear that the book belongs to the age after the
Exile; it is written in good Hebrew, but there are Aramaic
words which could only have been used by a Jew who lived
after the Exile, a time when Aramaic was becoming the speech
of the ordinary man in Judaea. But when one asks, how long
after the Exile, the authorities begin to differ. The conservative say ' *just* after the Exile ' and the radicals say ' in the
Greek period ' (i.e. after 333 B.C.). But on the whole 450 to
350 B.C. seems the most likely conjecture. Of the author we
know absolutely nothing beyond what we can guess from his
work. He must have been a Jew, well versed in the literature
of his people; and it seems likely that he lived, or at any rate
had lived, outside Palestine. He seems to have a special
knowledge of Egypt. Judging by the metaphors and illustra-
tions he uses in his book, we would say that he kept himself
well-informed about the social and political movements in
the world in which he lived.

Style

Before we try to estimate his style and literary qualities,
there is first need of some explanation about Hebrew poetry.
The scheme according to which all poetry in the Bible is
written is called *parallelism*. Hebrew poetry, instead of hav-

ing a rhyme in sound, to which we are accustomed, has a rhyme in sense. The second line in the verse does not echo the sound of the first one, it echoes its meaning. Thus the essence of Hebrew poetry is to express the same thought in different words in two consecutive lines. The lines, however, must be of a certain length; there is also a rhythm or beat, such as we are accustomed to in English verse. Very often the effect of this rhythm survives even being translated into English; here, for example, is a verse from Psalm 19, where we see both the three-beat rhythm, and the echoing of the sense in the second line:

> The heavens declare the glory of God
> And the firmament sheweth his handywork.

Here 'heavens' in the first line is paralleled by 'firmament' in the second; 'declare' in the first by 'sheweth' in the second, etc. We find exactly the same scheme in Job; but often it is much elaborated, and even more often it is obscured in the A.V. by mistranslation. For example, Job often gives us three consecutive parallel lines instead of two; thus in 3.4:

> Let that day be darkness;
> Let not God regard it from above;
> Neither let the light shine upon it.

A little farther down, in verse 12, however, we have a clear example of a two-lined verse:

> Why did the knees prevent me?
> Or why the breasts that I should suck?

and we can catch the three-beat rhythm of the Hebrew here also.

With a little practice, we can begin to distinguish the various lines for ourselves; this is greatly facilitated if it is pointed as poetry, as it is for instance in the R.V. But we must remember that sometimes, instead of the second line merely echoing the thought of the first, it develops it, though this is rarer in Job than in much other Hebrew literature. A good example is found in 38.3.

> Gird up now thy loins like a man;
> For I will demand of thee, and answer thou me.

This principle of Hebrew poetry is often important when we are trying to interpret an obscure passage; if it is not borne in mind, it will sometimes cause wrong exegesis. Here are two examples. If we took 31.36:

> Surely I would take it upon my shoulder
> And bind it as a crown to me,

too literally, we might imagine that Job is proposing to bind his protestation of innocence both on his shoulder and on his head, a difficult operation: whereas in fact he is merely saying how proudly he would wear it. Or again we might understand 18.10 wrongly:

> The snare is laid for him in the ground,
> And a trap for him in the way.

This does not mean that God has taken the precaution of laying two traps for the ungodly man, in case the first failed. It means that there surely is retribution waiting for him.

With these facts about Hebrew verse in mind, we will be able the better to appreciate the great poetry contained in Job. In many places unfortunately the poetry is obscured by the state of the text, but again and again it chimes forth through all the doubtful translation of the A.V., and we can enjoy the beauty of such verses as 38.7:

> When the morning stars sang together,
> And all the sons of God shouted for joy.

The Book of Job is the account of a conversation on a dung-hill, but for a backcloth the author uses heaven and earth, nature's phenomena and man's activities. He fetches his materials from all over the earth, and his poetry is enlivened by metaphors, figures and pictures from all sorts of different sources. Now he gives us little vignettes of the overthrow of empires (12.17-19), and now a startling glimpse of long-abandoned ruins of former civilizations in the desert

(3.14). He seems especially to love comparing God's power to an army; in 6.4 the terrors of God array themselves against Job; in 16.12-13, God's archers are marshalled against him, and they attack him like storm troops attacking a town. In 20.24 there is a grisly picture of God's weapon piercing the ungodly man's back and sticking out at his breast. In another place God is a lion (10.16); in 16.9 He seizes Job and worries him like a wild beast. Our author seems especially interested in the condition of the poor and outcast, and here he is in the true prophetic tradition, though he lacks the prophets' indignation. He gives us a terrible picture of the very poorest class in chapter 24, and in 30.3-7 we have his strange account of the gipsies or 'criminal tribes' of his day. Compare with these passages Job's almost morbid picture of social oppression, and the vices of city life, also in chapter 24; and the vivid picture of Job administering justice in the days of his prosperity in 29.7-17.

Our author can also take us up into the heights and make us realize the wonder and vastness of creation, and therefore of the Creator, very much as the Second Isaiah does. Think of that great glimpse of the stars and constellations in 9.8 and his pictures of the phenomena of the weather in 26.8-13 (Elihu, however, is even more interested in the weather—see chapter 37). It is in the thirty-eighth chapter, however, where God finally appears and overwhelms Job with questions about the wonders of creation, that our author's feeling for nature appears most clearly. One cannot help feeling his delight as he uses to the full this opportunity of writing poetry about nature; he does it with skill and enjoyment. His animals are so unnecessary to his argument, and yet so delightful in their context. Job has been talking about injustice and the government of the world: but what about the ostrich? How does he fit that into his scheme of things? And so the splendid procession of God's creatures goes on, the lioness, the raven, the aurochs (wild ox), the war-horse, the hawk—nearly all quite independent of man, and all worth describing by a poet for their own sake. As one reads that chapter, a comparison with

Milton seems to force itself on one. Like Milton, the author
of Job chose a legend, or a myth for his theme; like Milton,
he made it the vehicle for magnificent poetry; and like Milton,
it was also an expression of his deepest religious convictions.

One could go on almost indefinitely with a list of the pictures
and metaphors to be found in the Book of Job; they appear
suddenly, sometimes lasting only half a verse, like a momentary shot in a film. There is the tragic narrative of the traveller
dying of thirst in the desert (6.15); the garden (8.16); the tree
that grows again from a stump (14.7). Job describes his life
as passing rapidly like the imperial posts of the Persian Empire
(9.25); he tells his friends that they are quack doctors (13.4);
he describes God as treating him like an internee (13.27).
Zophar compares the life of the ungodly to a dream; and
draws a hideous picture of a man who suddenly discovers he
has swallowed poison (20.14). Job gives us a glimpse of what
is known as 'a beautiful funeral'. Tolstoy himself with his
mighty canvases is not more varied in his scope than our
author within his briefer medium.

Text and Editions

Suppose that for the first four hundred years after Chaucer
wrote, *The Canterbury Tales* had been handed on in hand-
written copies only, and that a final definitive copy had been
written out in 1851 by someone not well acquainted with Chau-
cerian English; and suppose that all our modern printed texts
of the *Tales* had to be taken from this one manuscript copy. If
you can make this act of imagination, you will have some idea
of the textual difficulties which are connected with the Book
of Job, except that, in the case of Job, the distance in time
between the Book leaving its author's hands, and of the making of the earliest copy we now have, is much greater than in
our imaginary example—more like one thousand five hundred
years instead of the four hundred or so we imagined. In the
case of the Book of Job, we have, however, some assistance
from a copy of the Greek translation. This copy was made
several centuries earlier than the oldest copy we possess in

Hebrew, but even then we must remember that the Greek and Hebrew languages belong to quite different families of speech and it is not always easy to guess what Hebrew word lies behind the Greek translation. Unfortunately the sensational finds of O.T. manuscripts recently made in Palestine did not contain any portion of the Book of Job.

All this preliminary information about manuscripts and translation is necessary to introduce us to the fact that the actual Hebrew text of the Book of Job is one of the most imperfect in the Old Testament. Apparently the highly poetical Hebrew in which it was written proved often incomprehensible to later scribes, who had to copy it; perhaps the fact that it was not dealing with matters frequently dealt with in the rest of the O.T. meant that there were many uncommon words in it. At any rate, all scholars are agreed that in very many places there are mistakes in the Hebrew text. What our surviving Hebrew manuscripts contain cannot in many places be what the author wrote. The problem is to guess, on the basis of these mistakes, what he did write. In other places, our difficulty arises not from mistakes in the text, but from the occurrence of words the meaning of which we simply do not know. Here one can sometimes turn to the Greek translator, who had access to sources of Hebrew learning now lost. But very often it is too plain that the Greek translator did not know the original meaning either, and anyway the only Greek translation we have seems to be an abbreviated version of the Book. We find sometimes that there just is no Greek translation to a verse or a phrase in the Hebrew. Consequently very often the only resource of scholars is to guess at the author's meaning. The Hebrew makes no sense, or uses a word whose meaning we do not know; the Greek can offer no help. We are driven back on the ingenuity of scholars.

This is no mean expedient; very often scholars make brilliant and convincing guesses as to what the original Hebrew was. (10.8, 15.23, 19.17 are good examples; see commentary on these places.) But it is an expedient of which both the A.V. and the R.V. have deliberately refused to avail themselves. In the case of the translators of the A.V. we can understand why; they believed that every word of the book had been directly inspired by the Holy Spirit, and hence were quite ready to see some mystic or hidden meaning in words which were on the surface meaningless. Also, excellent as was their scholarship in their generation, much more is known about Hebrew now than in 1611. Hence they could quite contentedly translate a Hebrew text that gave no sense or totally incongruous sense into an English that was almost as meaningless or quite as incongruous. But by a sad combination of circumstances, the translators of the R.V. produced a version that was almost as much bound to the literal sense or nonsense of the Hebrew text as was the A.V. The Committee that translated the R.V. decided all disputes about translation by a simple majority vote. But in matters of scholarship, it is often quality and not quantity that counts; the full implications of the critical study of the O.T. had not percolated into all the nooks and crannies of Hebrew scholarship by 1884 (when the R.V. was finished); the consequence was that, as Moffatt says: 'Good scholars on the Committee were often unable to get their proposals past the margin, where much of their best work is to be found.'

All this must serve as an apology for the extent to which this Commentary on the text is devoted to elucidating the actual meaning of any given verse. In many cases it must seem almost waste of time trying to find out what the original text was; after all, what does it matter what the author of the Elihu chapters originally wrote? It cannot have much relevance to the message of the Book of Job for us. But a word of warning is necessary. We *must* try and decide the meaning even of apparently unimportant passages, as there are those who delight in drawing curious and fantastic exegesis from the text of the O.T. and we must have our answer ready.

We must then confess with a recent scholar that 'of the English versions the A.V. appears at its worst in the Book of Job'. As far as recovering the original sense is concerned, the R.V. is not as good as one might expect. It has certain advantages over the A.V.: for one thing it points the verses as poetry; for another, it does indicate where the rendering is doubtful. The occurrence of one or more marginal alternatives usually indicates that the meaning is uncertain. Hence it is always worth while consulting the R.V. if you have one. But the Book of Job is one of the books in the Bible that most needs a modern translation, and Moffatt is at his best here, so Moffatt's modern translation should be used if possible, or else the American Revised Standard Version.

Of the English Commentaries probably the best is the Cambridge Bible edition, Davidson and Lanchester (C.U.P.). It is a little conservative and tends to moralize, but can be relied on for reasonable exegesis. Peake's Century Bible edition is also useful (Nelson). He is even more conservative, however, than Davidson and Lanchester. The Westminster Commentary (edited by Gibson, Methuen) is feeble, but of course a great deal better than no commentary at all. A good recent Commentary has been written by Kissane (Browne and Nolan), a Roman Catholic scholar. He has none of the timidity in matters of textual criticism which one sometimes associates with Roman Catholic exegesis of the Bible, and his translation is bold and refreshing. But he does not deal much with the wider aspects of the exegesis of the book. The best edition from the point of view of solid scholarship is Driver and Gray's Commentary in the International Critical Commentary Series (Longmans). It is very formidable in appearance with its array of technicalities, but it can be used profitably by those who have neither Hebrew nor Greek. It is impossible to say whether any of these books is in print at the moment at which you read this, but all can be picked up in second-hand book shops.

NOTE. Throughout this Commentary, A.V. means the Authorized Version of 1611, and R.V. means the Revised Version of 1884.

Where the A.V. prints a word in italics, it means that that word is not in the original Hebrew.

THE PROLOGUE
Chapters 1 and 2

Chapter 1

Uz in verse 1 is east of Palestine and north of Edom, and is therefore well into the desert. In verse 5 CURSED is literally 'blessed' in the Hebrew, and so also in verse 11 and in 2.5 and 9. This is a euphemism, for the meaning is certainly 'cursed'. The change may have been made by a later scribe who was shocked at the thought of cursing God. In this verse 5 also Job is described as sending for his children and making them undergo ritual purification before the sacrifice. All this is the traditional expression of the patriarch's righteousness.

In verse 6 we encounter SATAN; we must not think of him as the 'enemy of mankind' of Christian belief, but rather as one of the angels of God who has the invidious task of acting as counsel for the prosecution. He too belongs to the legend, and is ignored after chapter 2. In verse 15 the SABAEANS are a nomadic tribe. The FIRE OF GOD in verse 16 means lightning. When Job says in verse 21 NAKED SHALL I RETURN THITHER, he means 'to the earth', the common womb of all men. In verse 22 CHARGED GOD FOOLISHLY means 'accused God of injustice', as he explicitly does later on in the poem.

Chapter 2

In verse 4 SKIN FOR SKIN probably means: 'touch him himself, and you lose his allegiance'. You take away his life and he takes away his fidelity. In verse 7 we read of Job's SORE

BOILS; on the basis of this and of other indications about his disease later on, commentators usually diagnose his disease as elephantiasis. This is no doubt the nearest we can get to a definition of his disease, but we are reading poetry, not pathology, and a terrible malady is probably all that the author wishes to convey to us. In verse 10 Job replies to his wife's tempting words: 'SHALL WE RECEIVE GOOD AT THE HAND OF GOD, AND SHALL WE NOT RECEIVE EVIL?' This is still part of the legend, showing Job's extreme piety and obedience. In verse 11 the three friends are represented as all coming from neighbouring desert tribes. The Greek version assiduously supplies legendary details, but the only significance of the place-names is that they are neighbouring ones.

I

THE FIRST CYCLE OF SPEECHES
Chapters 3 to 11

Chapter 3 **Job's First Speech**

Impelled by his own experience, Job in this speech expounds the vanity of all life. This is Job's starting-point, utter hopelessness, as if the author wanted to start off from man's lowest point in his exploration of the relationship between God and man. Job at first asks only for rest, but his cry develops later into a plea for justice. With verses 3 to 12, compare Jeremiah 20.14 to 18, a passage which may well have inspired this one.

In verse 5 STAIN IT is probably not correct. 'Claim it for their own' (R.V.) is better. When Job speaks of BLACKNESS OF THE DAY he means eclipses and sandstorms. He wishes his birthday to be each year a day forgotten of God and marked by ill-omened happenings. In verse 6, for JOINED UNTO we should follow the A.V. margin 'rejoice among'. In verse 8, for THEIR MOURNING we must read 'Leviathan' (A.V. margin). The sense seems to be: 'Let those who by their enchantments can bring on an eclipse curse that day.' Leviathan was the snake-monster, who was perhaps believed to swallow up the sun when an eclipse occurred. This is a Hindu idea, not paralleled elsewhere in the O.T. but seems to give the best sense here. In verse 10 SORROW simply means 'this vale of tears'. WHY DID THE KNEES PREVENT ME? means probably 'why did my mother's knees receive me?'

In verses 13 to 19 Job gives us a picture of She'ol, the Hebrew name for the underworld where the dead go. It was believed that She'ol (which the A.V. usually translates as 'the pit') was a place of shadows and gloom, where the dead led a dreary life suitable to their bloodless state. There is no suggestion here of punishment of the wicked, or rewards for the righteous. The pathos of Job's words is that he prefers even the gloom of She'ol to his present condition. In verse 14 instead of DESOLATE PLACES many scholars translate 'pyramids'. When the author of the Book of Job wrote, the Great Pyramid was about two thousand years old; we have already seen that our author probably knew something of Egypt. In verse 24 BEFORE I EAT is not satisfactory sense; perhaps the meaning of the verse is: 'I have my sighs for food and my moans for drink.' Translate all past tenses in verse 26 as presents: Job is describing his present condition.

Chapters 4 and 5   Eliphaz's First Speech

Eliphaz propounds the orthodox doctrine, neatly summarized in 4.7 and 8, that the righteous never ultimately lose their material prosperity in this life and conversely that the unrighteous are always ultimately ruined in this life. In chapter 5 he offers a guarantee that the righteous will be materially preserved by God in this life; in the course of the centuries many Christians in adversity have found comfort in chapter 5. But in order to use it thus it has to be interpreted in a spiritual sense, which quite transcends Eliphaz's meaning. In 4.12-17 Eliphaz reinforces his argument by describing a religious experience of his own. The experience when related turns out to be a simple apprehension of the awe and terrifying majesty of God. It may have convinced Eliphaz that you cannot argue with God, but it does nothing to prove that the guilty are inevitably punished in this life.

Chapter 4

In verse 6 we must follow the R.V.:

> Is not thy fear of God thy confidence,
> And thy hope the integrity of thy ways?

In verses 10 and 11 the Hebrew offers no less than five different words for LION! In verse 12, instead of A LITTLE THEREOF we must read 'a whisper thereof' (R.V.). In verse 16, follow the A.V. margin, and for THERE WAS SILENCE, AND I HEARD A VOICE read 'I heard a still voice'; cf. 1 Kings 19.12. In verse 19 HOUSES OF CLAY means 'earthly bodies', and we should read 'like the moth' rather than BEFORE THE MOTH. In verse 20 the sense is that their life, like a moth's, lasts but a day. In the first half of verse 21 it is on the whole better to follow the R.V. translation:

> Is not their tent-cord plucked up within them?

Chapter 5

In verse 1 the sense is that it is no good appealing to the angels (A.V. Saints), since God treats even them as sinners. The possibility mentioned here of making prayer to the angels shows that the Book must have been written after the Exile, as we do not find such ideas before the period of Persian rule. The meaning of verse 2 is that if you allow yourself to be exacerbated by the blows of fate you will only shorten your days—not much comfort for one who longed for death! The GATE in verse 4 is the law-court of those times; it was at the city-gate that oriental justice was meted out; the children of the unrighteous lose their property through unsuccessful litigation. Verse 5 is one of the many verses in Job where all that we can say with certainty is that the A.V. is wrong. The following translation has fair probability:

> Their sheaf the poor taketh,
> And they, thirsty, shall yearn for their wealth.

In verses 6 and 7 is Eliphaz saying that disaster is not something that happens arbitrarily but is the result of one's own actions, as verse 6 suggests; or is he saying that calamity is the inevitable lot of all mankind, as verse 7 suggests? The text, the meaning of the text, and the general import of this part of Eliphaz's speech are all uncertain.

The first half of verse 13 is quoted by Paul in I Corinthians 3.19. Paul uses it to rebuke those intellectuals who refused to accept the foolishness of the Cross. After the full revelation of God in Jesus Christ such a rebuke is justified; but Eliphaz uses it to rebuke Job. Now Job was, after all, himself searching for a deeper knowledge of God's nature, at a time when God had not as yet given anything like a full or sufficient revelation of Himself. Those who sought in this way before the coming of our Lord are referred to in I Peter 1.10-13: 'Of which salvation the prophets have enquired and searched diligently, who prophesied of the grace that should come unto you.' Surely the author of Job might be numbered in this succession. FROWARD in the second half of verse 13 means 'tortuous, perverse'. By CARRIED HEADLONG Eliphaz means that their plans mature too early and thus are ruined. In verse 15 FROM THE SWORD, FROM THEIR MOUTH is wrong;

> He saveth the guileless from the sword

is a fair attempt at a rendering. In verse 19 SIX, YEA SEVEN is simply a Hebrew idiom meaning 'many troubles', cf. Matthew 18.21-22. In verse 23 IN LEAGUE WITH THE STONES OF THE FIELD means that the stones do not lie about the field and prevent cultivation.

Chapters 6 and 7   **Job's Response to Eliphaz**

Chapter 6

In verse 3 (second half) we must follow the R.V. in translating:

> Therefore have my words been rash.

Job admits for a moment that he has overstepped the limit, but it does not inhibit him from overstepping it even more in these two chapters. In verse 4 THE POISON WHEREOF DRINKETH UP MY SPIRIT should be:

> The poison whereof my spirit drinketh up

as in the R.V. The meaning of verse 5 is: 'I am not making
a fuss about nothing, any more than the animals do when *they*
cry out.' Similarly we must understand verse 6 as: 'My crying out is as natural as is man's repugnance to tasteless food.'
UNSAVOURY in the A.V. is the equivalent of our modern 'in-
sipid'. WHITE OF AN EGG in this verse probably has to be
replaced by the much less vivid 'slime of purslane', the juice
of a tasteless plant. Both the A.V. and the R.V. renderings
of verse 7 are astray; the following is a likely guess:

> My soul refuseth to be quiet;
> It is agitated by the sickness of my flesh.

In verses 9 and 10 Job asks for death and thereby implicitly
accuses God of injustice. Compare Elijah's complaint in
I Kings 19.4. On the other hand, in verse 10 we seem to find
an appeal to the God of moral law. Job is appealing from
God the tormentor and author of his disease to the moral
God, whose commandments he has obeyed: the situation is
remarkably like that in a play by Aeschylus, a Greek
dramatist, who may very well have been contemporary with
our author. In the Greek dramatist's *Prometheus Bound*,
Prometheus, the victim of Zeus's tyranny, constantly appeals
to divine justice, which he believes is on his side. The difference between the two works is that Job believes that ultimately the two aspects of God must be reconciled. In verse
10, instead of HARDEN MYSELF IN SORROW; LET HIM NOT SPARE,
we must follow the R.V. and read:

> Yea I would exult in pain that spareth not.

Job is ready to face any pain if death with conscious innocence
awaits him at the end of it.
    In verse 14, the A.V. is unsatisfactory. Here is Moffatt's
translation, which seems the best:

> Friends should be kind to a despairing man,
> Or he will give up faith in the Almighty.

In verse 15 Job compares his friends to mountain torrents,

excellent in winter when the melting snow fills them, but they just disappear in the hot season when one most needs them. The subject changes in verse 18 from the streams to the travellers, though this is not indicated in the A.V. where, instead of THE PATHS OF THEIR WAY ARE TURNED ASIDE, we should read:

> Caravans divert their way.

TEMA and SHEBA in verse 19 are desert stations.

Job, in verse 21, makes the comparison more pointed than the A.V. would lead one to imagine. We should read:

> For now ye have become unto me like these (brooks).

The real gist of Job's complaint about his friends is that they have not taken his side against God. The glory of Job's position is that he is determined to have personal encounter with God. God should meet him, and he God, as a person. The conventional piety of his friends tended to treat God as remote and not to be argued with. In verse 25, for FORCIBLE read 'pleasant'. Job wants a straight answer, but can get nothing out of Eliphaz's arguments. By using WIND in verse 26 to describe his own words, Job shows that he does not want to be taken too seriously yet. In verse 29 the A.V. translation seems meaningless: let us follow the R.V.:

> Return, I pray you, let there be no injustice;
> Yea, return again, my cause is righteous.

The sense of verse 30 is: 'Can't you trust my judgement when I tell you that it is not my sins I am suffering for?'

Chapter 7

For APPOINTED TIME in verse 1 read the A.V. margin 'warfare'. Verse 4 has to be slightly altered, so as to read:

> When I lie down, I say, when shall I arise?
> And as often as evening comes, I am full of tossings, etc.

In verse 7 he addresses God directly for the first time, a significant development in his attitude. In verse 8 read:

Thou shalt look for me, and I shall not be

—even God will not be able to find him. We are reminded in verse 12 that God controlled the sea monster (not WHALE) Tiamat, when He first created the world (cf. 38.8-11, Jeremiah 5.22 and 31.35; Psalm 104.9) Job asks ironically whether God is treating him in the same way as He dealt with Tiamat. Notice the author's willingness to use the mythology of his day. We must follow the R.V. in verse 20:

If I have sinned, what do I unto thee?

Job only admits venial and perhaps inadvertent sins. In the second half of the verse, instead of PRESERVER we should read 'watcher'. The verb is often used elsewhere in the O.T. of God's providential care; here by irony care is interpreted as spying. Omit IN THE MORNING in verse 21. It is not in the Hebrew.

In this chapter, Job speaks again of his sufferings, but this time he thinks of himself as a representative of suffering humanity. The whole chapter is really an exposition of the standing of man before God. Job realizes the full awfulness of the unique position in which man is placed. The very fact of his protest against the relationship in which he finds himself shows how infinitely deeper his thought is than that of his friends. Those well-meaning commentators who try to apologize for this chapter by saying that Job's sufferings have made him a little hasty, have missed the point altogether. Verse 17. with its cry of WHAT IS MAN? gives the keynote to the second half of the chapter, which is a protest against the positive, almost aggressive character of God's relation to man. He parodies Psalm 8, where we find wondering gratitude at God's care for man. Job, far from admiring God for this condescension in so blessing man with a prominent place in the universe, bitterly asks why God bothers to worry such an insignificant insect. This is in fact the complementary truth to Psalm 8 : man is both king of the universe and a frail reed; monarch of infinite space and bounded in a nutshell; the crown of God's creation, and unworthy of God's attention.

When Job calls God 'thou watcher of men' (v. 20) in a hostile sense, he reveals the state of mind of one who knows the living and personal God, but not His grace and love. The cry of 'let me alone' is a very frequent one throughout the history of Christianity and before it. Compare Jonah 1.3; 4.3; also Saul of Tarsus kicking against the pricks. A modern example can be found in the story of the youth Sundar Singh, who publicly burnt a copy of the Bible in a frenzy of rage against the faith which he was on the verge of accepting. In the New Testament we read of evil spirits crying out against our Lord before they were overcome; cf. Mark 5.7. What a testimony to the integrity of the Bible, the witness to the nature and acts of God, that it should find a place for this feeling of protest against His inescapable presence! How remote from conventional piety is this chapter and how absurd it makes it to use the epithet 'patient' of Job!

Chapter 8   Bildad's First Speech
'Those who suffer must have sinned: those who sin receive their due reward.' So runs Bildad's simple argument. In verse 4 he politely says: IF THY CHILDREN HAVE SINNED . . . but he obviously believes they have. We must read not HYPOCRITE in verse 13, but 'godless' (R.V.). Verse 14 gives us a good example of a place where the scholar's guess is obviously right. A very small change in the Hebrew makes the first half of the verse run:

Whose hope is gossamer.

SEETH THE PLACES OF STONES in verse 17 is improbable: 'pierceth the place of stones' is better.

Chapters 9 and 10   Job's Response to Bildad
Chapter 9
The question HOW SHOULD MAN BE JUST WITH GOD? (verse 2)

when asked elsewhere in the O.T. means that a man cannot
stand before Him because of sin. Here it is a man assumed
to be 'perfect' who is speaking, and he feels the overwhelming power of God which prevents his case being heard. This
might seem a retrogression from the high moral terms in
which the prophets had thought of man's relation with God
(one cannot imagine Isaiah making out a case for himself
against God). But we must remember that Job is all the time
seeking for the next step in God's revelation. He is a perfect
man as the prophets would define righteousness, and yet he
must seek for that personal contact with God which he lacks.
This next revelation, which would answer all Job's need,
comes only with our Lord Himself. In verse 3 we find the
conception of a man contending with God. It is not exactly
paralleled anywhere else in the Bible; but compare Micah 6.2,
where God contends with Israel, calling nature to witness; cf.
also Genesis 32.24-30. The friends did not like the idea of
such a contention, as it seemed impious to question God; but
it really means that Job is striving for a more fully personal
and just idea of God than that which they hold.

Elsewhere in the O.T. the activity of God in nature is often
portrayed, but nearly always that activity is looked on as pur-
posive and beneficent. Here (verses 5 to 13) is a picture of
the world, in opposition to that of Eliphaz in 5.9-27, in
which the destructive forces of nature are emphasized. It is
more ruthless but also more true than the sentimental picture
of the 'God of the open air', whose activities seem to provide
nothing more than a pleasant setting for human life. It is
indeed not easy to see the beneficent hand of God in every
phenomenon of nature; whoever does so easily is taking a very
superficial view. In verse 9, behind the phrase CHAMBERS OF
THE SOUTH is probably hidden the name of some constellation. The A.V. rendering of verse 13 is not satisfactory. We
should substitute the following:

> Even a god cannot stay his anger;
> The helpers of Rahab do stoop under him.

The reference is once more to the primitive creation-myth, in which God defeated the chaos-dragon (here called Rahab) and her horde of attendant deities. The Babylonian account of this battle actually mentions these HELPERS. If even semi-divine beings cannot resist God, how can Job? Once again our author uses contemporary mythology; it may be part of the patriarchal setting which he has deliberately chosen.

We find in verses 14 to 21 that the main emphasis has shifted from the problem of suffering to the problem of man's relation to God. It never shifts back. As far as the problem of innocent suffering is concerned Eliphaz has already given the only two answers which are to be found in the Book: 'Suffering is disciplinary' (5.17 and 18), and 'Trust God without asking questions' (5.8 and 9). But Job has now moved on to the deeper ground of man's relation to God. It is in this section that he is most prophetic of the N.T. revelation. He longs for the relationship of divine humility and grace which was manifested in Christ. The true answer to his need is to be found in such a passage as Phil. 2.5-8. In verse 15 we should read not JUDGE but 'adversary at law'. Job says it would be no use arguing his case. He would have to throw himself on the mercy of his adversary (God). CALLED in verse 16 is not exactly right; the Hebrew word is a legal one: 'summonsed' is perhaps better. The meaning of verse 20 is not that Job admits his guilt, but that God unjustly insists on treating him as guilty.

In verses 22 to 24, Job accuses God of using His divine power to annihilate His innocent adversary, and concludes that this injustice is equally demonstrated in God's government of the world. It is interesting to notice that when you accept the opposite principle, that is, that God has stripped Himself of His awe and come down to man's level, you then understand the true secret of God's government of the world. Where there is innocent suffering God does not cause it, but suffers in the sufferer. There is a story about St. Vincent de Paul, which relates how he once brought to some pious ladies, who helped him in his work amongst the poor, an illegitimate baby which had been abandoned by its parents. The ladies suggested that God might have meant the baby to be left to die as a punishment for its parents' sin. St. Vincent de Paul replied: 'When God wants dying to be done for sin He sends His own Son to do it.' It is also true that when man sees that God has come down and stripped Himself of His overwhelming power, the innocence and uprightness which man claims for himself (cf. Job 9.21) has gone too, and he can only say with Peter: 'Depart from me, for I am a sinful man, O Lord.' (Luke 5.8.) In verse 22 for THIS ONE THING we must follow the R.V.'s.

It is all one.

Seeing that there is no such thing as a reward for piety, Job feels that he can say what he likes. THE SCOURGE in verse 23 means some great disaster involving multitudes. We must emend the last clause of verse 24 to read:

If it be not he (who is responsible for this state of affairs) then who is it?

How can anyone who has read these outrageous accusations maintain the legend of the pious and patient Job?

In writing of the POST in verse 25, the author has in mind the swift couriers of the Persian Imperial Service. This is, of course, a gross anachronism if we take the patriarchal background seriously. SWIFT SHIPS in verse 26 is incorrect; 'ships of reed', R.V. Margin, is right; these were found in Egypt, and this is another slight indication of our author's interest in that country. In verse 29:

If I am to be held guilty . . .

is a better translation. DAYSMAN in verse 33 means 'umpire, arbiter', Jesus Christ was not a daysman in this sense; when God met the need to which Job gives expression He went beyond this conception of arbiter, and came as friend and redeemer. The consequence is that man abandons his own claim to righteousness, seeing that the whole relationship has

been taken out of the sphere of law altogether. The sense of
the last clause in verse 35 seems to be: 'for I am not conscious of any guilt in myself.'

Chapter 10
For a Christian utterance about as similar to the thoughts
expressed in verses 1 to 7 as a Christian's could be, compare
a poem of Gerard Manley Hopkins, which begins:

> Thou art indeed just, Lord, if I contend
> With Thee; but, Sir, so what I plead is just.
> Why do sinners' ways prosper? And why must
> Disappointment all I endeavour end?
> Wert Thou my enemy, oh Thou my friend,
> How wouldst Thou worse, I wonder, than Thou dost
> Defeat, thwart me? . . .

The whole poem is worth reading in this context. In verse 1
of this chapter, FOR I WILL LEAVE MY COMPLAINT UPON MY-
SELF, we must read:

> I will give free course to my complaint, R.V.

Gerard Manley Hopkins again has a poem which begins with
words that might almost be inspired by verses 8 and 9 of this
chapter:

> Thou mastering me
> God! Giver of breath and bread;
> World's strand, sway of the sea;
> Lord of living and dead;
> Thou hast bound bones and veins in me, fastened me flesh,
> And after it almost unmade, what with dread,
> Thy doing: and dost Thou touch me afresh?
> Over again I feel Thy finger and find Thee.
>   (*Wreck of the Deutschland*, verse 1)

In verse 8, instead of YET THOU DOST DESTROY ME we should
translate:

> Afterwards thou turnest and destroyest me.

Verses 10 to 12 describe procreation, the formation of the fœtus in the womb, and finally its birth, which is indicated by the word LIFE in verse 12; compare Psalm 139.13-16. The meaning of verse 13 is: 'and yet all the time you had this sinister purpose in mind for me.' The following verses, 14 to 17, describe God's sinister programme. They should be read with a ' that ' in front of each clause:

Thy purpose is that if I sin . . . that if I be wicked, etc.

Thus Job does not really admit his guilt here. He only says that it does not matter whether he sins or not, God persecutes him all the same. Job seems to understand almost everything about the nature of God except that He is love. Christian poets have used language very similar to this to express God's determined love for man. Compare the hymn: 'O Love that will not let me go', and Francis Thompson's *The Hound of Heaven*. In verse 15, we should probably emend the last part to read:

I am full of confusion
And drunk with affliction.

The first words of verse 16 FOR IT INCREASETH are wrong. Possibly

And thou exaltest thyself

is right. The lower Job's state, the more insulting is God. WITNESSES, in verse 17, mean Job's sufferings, interpreted as signs of God's displeasure. In the next line CHANGES AND WAR ARE AGAINST ME, the word translated CHANGES can mean 'a period of service', so a good translation is:

A renewal of hard service is my lot.

Notice how much the figure of the law-court haunts our author's mind. There is never any question, throughout the book, of Job ceasing to believe in God; on the contrary, the more outrageous his language, the more intimate and personal does his relation to God become.

Chapter 11 **Zophar's First Speech**

Zophar, for all his saying that Job cannot understand God (verses 7 and 8)—no one can—is really claiming to understand God's purposes for Job. He claims that Job is having to undergo suffering for the reason already suggested: he has sinned (verses 13 and 14). It is noteworthy that when God does appear, He does not convict Job of any specific sins, though He rebukes the great sin Job committed in trying to plead his own righteousness to God. Certainly there is no indication that the author intended us to imagine that Job's sufferings were, in God's sight, due to previous sin.

One editor, commenting on verses 4 to 6, suggests that Zophar is dealing with the problem of what a man's conscience tells him about his guilt, and what his external circumstances indicate, going on to suggest how one's conscience may be enlightened about one's condition. But this is not the point: Job is not at all worried about whether his own conscience is speaking the truth or not. He has no doubts on that score. He is concentrating all the time on what is the fundamental problem for him, God's nature. Zophar, as all the friends try to do in their different ways, attempts to reduce the problem to dimensions which he understands. For Zophar, Job is simply a man who will not acknowledge his own guilt. Having got Job classified, as he believes, he is able in verses 13 to 20 to preach an uplifting sermon consisting of moral platitudes. Verse 6 is very difficult to get the right meaning from: THAT THEY ARE DOUBLE TO THAT WHICH IS does not convey much meaning. Moffatt translates the first two clauses thus:

> Unfolding all the mysteries of his wisdom,
> The marvel of his methods.

KNOW THEREFORE, etc., is delightfully suitable to Zophar's pugnacious style, but is it what the Hebrew means? Probably not; we cannot rescue the exact meaning. 'God is punishing your iniquity,' is perhaps the general sense. Not BY SEARCHING in verse 7, but:

> Canst thou reach the limit of God?

It is not the difficulty of finding God that Zophar emphasizes, but the impossibility of exhausting His wisdom. In the end, it is neither his own exasperated protests that satisfy Job, nor his friends' arguments, but a revelation from the side of God Himself. In verse 11 WILL HE NOT THEN CONSIDER IT? is probably an incorrect translation. Perhaps 'without considering it' is the best suggestion. In that case, the argument of verses 11 and 12 would seem to be 'God knows men's hearts all right; He knows all about wickedness, though He does not make the fuss about it that you do. Even you will come to understand in the end, stupid though you are.' The suggestion contained in verse 16, that Job will forget all his troubles, is amazingly superficial; as if one could forget the death of all one's children. But it is no more superficial than the Epilogue. In verse 18, instead of DIG ABOUT THEE a better rendering is:

Look about thee (with satisfaction).

II

THE SECOND CYCLE OF SPEECHES
Chapters 12 to 20

Chapters 12 to 14 **Job Replies to Zophar, and Elaborates his Complaint**

Chapter 12

In this chapter Job stresses that only when a man is in trouble does he begin to see that there is a problem, i.e. that the wicked prosper. Job cannot explain the principles on which God works, but he does maintain the unexpectedness of His action in history. The friends thought they knew the principles on which God orders history. Job argues that they do not, and gives, in verses 14 to 25, a catalogue of the strange reverses of history which are the work of God. Compare Daniel 2.20 to 21. Once more Job refutes conventional arguments and seems to speak blasphemously about God, but in reality he is going beyond the outlook of conventional religion to a deeper vision of God. He prepares the way to this deeper understanding by maintaining that God's action in history cannot be predicted, and by this insistence, he leaves the realms of the conventional Jewish theory.

In verse 2 YE ARE THE PEOPLE means:

Ye are the people of intelligence.

AND HE ANSWERETH HIM in verse 4 is not good sense.

Who calleth upon God and answereth God's call

is a possible translation and fits the meaning well. Verse 5
is badly mishandled in the A.V. The R.V. is good:

> In the thought of him that is at ease, there is contempt for
> misfortune.

INTO WHOSE HAND GOD BRINGETH ABUNDANTLY in verse 6 is not
correct. It seems to be a description of people for whom
might is right. Translate it as:

> Even he that bringeth his god in his hand.

In verses 7 to 12, Job appeals to the universal experience of
all creation that might is right. 'Nature red in tooth and
claw', as well as innumerable generations of men, confirms
this, says Job. The meaning of verse 11 is 'you must accept
the conclusions of experience'. Verses 13 to 25 provide a
magnificent description of God in His purely destructive
activities, viewed, as far as Job is concerned, as a purely
a-moral agent. One could illustrate every verse from the
history of the twentieth century. When properly balanced by
the other elements in God's character, it forms a useful anti-
dote to the popular idea of the uninterrupted upward march
of man. In verse 16 THE DECEIVED AND THE DECEIVER means
perhaps the mob-orator and the mob whom he inflames. THE
BONDS OF KINGS in verse 18, are the bonds the kings impose.
THE GIRDLE in the same verse is the loincloth of the day-
labourer. God makes kings into coolies, doing forced labour.
MIGHTY in verse 19 is more exactly 'the firmly-established',
i.e. the respectable. Job attributes to God the fall of the
bourgeoisie!

Chapter 13
  Verses 1 to 12: these verses abundantly justify the view
taken in the last chapter. In them Job reproves his friends
for misrepresenting God, even though by their misrepresenta-
tion they make God appear more agreeable than Job's reading
of history leads him to apprehend. From this we may certainly conclude that Job had not abandoned belief in a con-

sistent and moral God; what he was striving for was a deeper understanding of that God. In clearing the ground for this deeper understanding he appears to his friends to be verging on the blasphemous.

FORGERS in verse 4 is better translated 'plasterers'; they are like ignorant physicians who plaster over a festering wound; cf. Jer. 6.14. What Job is doing in verses 4 and 7 and 8 is accusing the friends of showing favouritism to God, blaming Job and exonerating his Persecutor. What amazing boldness! Once more, the arguments of the infidel (though Job is no infidel) are put in the mouth of a biblical character. Perhaps most of us have heard the taunt at one time or another: 'You church people are sentimentalists who shut your eyes to the hard facts.' Verse 9 shows that all the time Job is keeping in the back of his mind a conception of God as just, as one who can be appealed to against His own injustice. The second half of verse 9 OR AS ONE MAN MOCKETH, etc., is mistranslated in the A.V. and should read as:

Will it be well when He shall put you to the test?

This appeal from God to God comes out more clearly later. Of course Job's half-formulated notion of God just and God unjust is wide of the mark; but by his very aberrations Job is perhaps groping after the thought of a complex nature in God. Later on, when the full nature of God was revealed in Christ, such a complexity appears much more convincingly worked out in the doctrine of the Trinity, and we can understand that His justice is but one aspect of His love. The sense of verses 10 and 11 is 'God will not approve of your favouring Him.' In verse 12 REMEMBRANCES is better translated 'maxims'. BODIES in the same verse is also wrong. It means 'defences' (R.V.).

Verses 13 to 28: Job's insistence on 'having it out' with God, treating God as a person who can be faced, is the glory of this Book. Job's desire was a good and a right one, but its fulfilment has a very different result from what he expected. When the Christian meets a God who has removed His awe and revealed His ways, he loses the desire to make out a case for himself, as he is overwhelmed with the glory shown on the Cross.

WHEREFORE in verse 14, should be omitted. This gives the sense: 'I will take my flesh in my teeth', i.e. Job will risk all and speak the truth. THOUGH HE SLAY ME, YET WILL I TRUST HIM: this magnificent line in the A.V. is unfortunately not an accurate translation. Moffatt renders the verse well:

> He may kill me—what else can I expect?
> But I will maintain my innocence to his face.

In verse 16 not HE but 'This' (R.V.). Job somehow hopes that his own integrity will prove his salvation. This goes far to atone for the disappointment of verse 15. Job is reverting to that dim presentiment of another aspect of God, one where his integrity will be of value. CALL, ANSWER, SPEAK in verse 22 are all legal terms. Job is summonsing God into court. This is the first great challenge; the last occurs at the end of chapter 31. WRITEST BITTER THINGS AGAINST ME in verse 26 refers to the legal indictment which Job believes God has drawn up against him. Verse 27 seems to give us three pictures of prisoners: (1) a man who is in the stocks, (2) a man under police surveillance, (3) a man under house arrest. The last clause should be translated:

> Thou drawest a line about the soles of my feet (R.V.).

The first clause of verse 28 must be changed to:

> though I am like a rotten thing that consumeth. . . .

At the end of this chapter God has failed to appear in response to Job's summons, so Job proceeds to enlarge his complaint against God in the absence of the defendant.

Chapter 14

Job, in pursuing his enquiry into the relationship between God and man, is eventually brought up against the fact that there can be no ultimately satisfactory fellowship between the two unless man is destined by God to be the heir of eternity.

Neither Job nor anyone in the Bible thinks of man as *necessarily* immortal.[1] Eternal life is thought of both by Job, in his request to God for a respite and further meeting, and by N.T. writers, as a gift coming out of God's good pleasure. Hence it follows that when the true relationship between God and man is declared in Jesus Christ, eternal life is at the same time given to man in this relationship.

The relevance of verse 4 to the context is not at all clear; it is not sin, but impermanency, that Job is lamenting. Perhaps we might translate:

Oh that the clean perished not with the unclean.

Notice that verse 12 is not a prophecy of the general resurrection at the last day, but implies that death is an everlasting condition. We find in verse 13 traces of the double personality in God which we have previously noticed in Job's thought. On the one hand God's wrath comes on Job; on the other God is asked to hide Job from the wrath. It is illogical, but it is a stage in the development of the understanding of God's true nature. In verse 15 Job maintains that only if he has hope of life beyond the grave can he truly meet God; but he inclines to think that there is no hope of such a life. Compare with this passage I Cor. 15.19: 'If in this life only we have hope in Christ, we are of all men most miserable.' In a sense the whole Bible is the story of God's meeting with man, and in that story this chapter represents a remarkably deep insight. Verses 14 to 17 present a problem: they might be understood as a mere rejection of the possibility of a future life; in that case CHANGE in verse 14 simply means 'death', and verses 16 to 17 mean that God registers Job's every sin. But in view of verse 15, which certainly refers to some hypothetical future happy relationship between Job and God, it is better to take these verses as Job's indulgence in the speculation that God might let a man die and then revive him again. If so, the first clause of verse 14 must run:

If a man might die, and come to life again!

[1] But the doctrine is found in the Book of Wisdom in the Apocrypha.

And verse 16 will be:

> For then thou wouldest number my steps (in loving care).
> Thou wouldest not watch for my sin.

Verse 17 will then refer to forgetting and forgiving, and not to recording his sin. If this second interpretation be right, the older commentators are to some extent justified in treating this passage as a prophecy of the resurrection. But it is not an inspired, nor even a confident prophecy. Rather it is a pathetic speculation, a day-dream which he dismisses in the verses that follow. Verse 19 should read, in its second clause:

> The overflowings thereof wash away the dust of the earth
>   (R.V.).

In verse 22 we apparently meet the gruesome idea that the dead man in some way in She'ol feels the decay of his corpse. This was no doubt a popular belief of the day. In its context it adds a final touch to the black picture of human misery which Job delineates.

The topic of the transitory nature of man's existence is frequently found in Greek and Roman literature. But when the classical writers attained a belief in a life after the grave, they did so purely on moral grounds. Plato's reincarnation theory, for example, is fundamentally an attempt to readjust the injustices of this life. Our Hebrew writer, on the other hand, in this lament for man's impermanence is speaking not so much of moral rights and wrongs as in meditation on man's relation to God. He laments man's ephemeral nature primarily because it makes impossible man's perfect communion with the living God. This is what the Sadducees who did not believe in a future life failed to understand. Our Lord's one argument for the future life in reply to them is highly significant: 'I am the God of Abraham, and the God of Isaac, and the God of Jacob. He is not the God of the dead, but the God of the living.' (Mark 12.18-27.) Our Lord is saying that if you call God the God of Abraham, Isaac and Jacob, you assume that these are living persons. Because God is a God who deals with persons, He must also be a God who grants eternal life. Compare in this connection the way in which the great Christian thinker, Blaise Pascal, described his mystical vision of God: 'The God of Abraham, of Isaac and of Jacob, and not the God of the philosophers.'

Chapter 15   Eliphaz's Second Speech

Eliphaz thinks that, unless you believe God punishes iniquity and rewards virtue in this life, the whole foundation of fear towards God is gone. Religious reformers, or religious men of an original bent of mind, very often meet the criticism that they are lacking in reverence towards God. Throughout the Book, Job's friends keep putting forward the stock arguments founded on conventional religious attitudes. These cannot satisfy Job, since they do not spring from that personal communion with God towards which he is pressing.

The first clause of verse 5 should run:

> Thine iniquity teacheth thy mouth.

The meaning of verse 8 is: 'Do you claim a monopoly of wisdom?' In this second speech Eliphaz is markedly rougher with Job than he was in his more tactful first speech. In verse 11 the CONSOLATIONS OF GOD are apparently the helpful words of advice offered by Eliphaz and his friends. IS THERE ANY SECRET THING WITH THEE? in the second half of the verse must be amended to:

> and the word that dealeth gently with thee (R.V.).

The general sense of verses 18 and 19 is that Eliphaz's teaching belongs to an ancient tradition coming down from purer times. The reference to strangers in verse 19 may be to the pre-exilic days when Samaria was inhabited by pure and orthodox Jews only, and not by the mixed population planted there at the time of the exile. If so, it is a most appropriate sentiment in Eliphaz's mouth, and the fact that our author attributes it to one of the friends, whose orthodoxy he represents as out of date, suggests a sympathy of thought between him and the author of the Book of Jonah.

Eliphaz's picture, portrayed in verse 20 onward, of the evil man as tormented by a bad conscience, is typical of the efforts pious people have made in all ages to explain away the prosperity of the wicked. Perhaps the wicked man does not suffer material misfortunes, they may say, but imagine what he suffers in his conscience! In fact, some of the most obviously wicked people in history have been the most obviously immune from remorse. For example, what Hitler suffered from in his last days was not a bad conscience, but the consequences of his own self-exaltation. Every fresh failure had to be explained not as his own fault, but as treachery on the part of his subordinates. This was indeed the wrath of God, but very different from the state of mind which Eliphaz describes. The N.T. writers, in this respect more realistic than later legend, made no attempt to follow up the career of Caiaphas after the Crucifixion. But contrast their treatment of Judas. The second clause of verse 20 should read:

and the number of years that is laid up for the oppressor.

The last years of the wicked are to be spent under the tyrant's yoke. A very slight alteration in the Hebrew of verse 23 changes HE WANDERETH ABROAD FOR BREAD SAYING: WHERE IS IT? into:

Destined as food for the vultures.

Verse 26 described the wicked man as hurling himself to his destruction against a well-armed God. With verse 27 compare Psalm 73.7; fatness in the O.T. is often a sign of overweening pride. The wicked man is described in verse 28 as dwelling in desolate cities, either because he has ruined them by his oppression, or because he has the audacity to dwell in places which God has destroyed. The last clause of verse 29, NEITHER SHALL HE PROLONG THE PERFECTION THEREOF, etc., is a guess by the A.V. translators. A better guess is:

neither shall his full ears of corn bend to the earth.

We must also change the last clause of verse 30: AND BY THE

BREATH OF HIS MOUTH SHALL HE GO AWAY. Perhaps the best alternative is Moffatt's

> his fruit is whirled off by the wind.

The meaning of verse 33 is that just as a destructive wind shakes off the unripe fruit from the vine and the flower from the olive, so the wicked man will not come to any good.

Chapters 16 and 17 **Job's Response to Eliphaz's Second Speech**

Chapter 16

In this chapter, Job passes from complaints of the uselessness of his friends' sentiments, and the experiences which they cite, to his already well-worn theme, the hostile attitude which he believes God assumes toward him. It is his relation to God that really concerns him. He has experienced in his earlier life the benevolence of God, and now, the greatest and last torment in his chapter of suffering, he feels God has deserted him and has become inaccessible. God is to him an actively hostile force. Our Lord's words on the cross: ' My God, my God, why hast thou forsaken me? ' reflect a similar experience of separation; but unlike Job, He is not led by suffering into the bitter and bewildering experience of feeling that God is His tormentor.

Verse 7 is very uncertain in the Hebrew; both A.V. and R.V. are wrong. The following is a fair guess:

> He hath wearied me out and appalled me,
> And all my calamity hath seized hold of me.

It refers to God's attack on Job. The next verse also must be emended to:

> It (calamity) hath been a witness against me and risen up
>   against me.
> My leanness testifieth to my face.

Job claims that God shows He holds him guilty by the disease He has sent. The figure in verse 9 is of a wild beast, to which

God in His pursuit of Job is compared.   Read the first clause
as:

He teareth Himself in His wrath and pursueth me.

First the beast bursts out in wrath, then he pursues his victim,
then he stands over it ready to tear it to pieces.   What an
amazingly bold figure to apply to God!   Verse 10 may be
an insertion by some later copyist from Psalm 22.13.   If not,
it refers to the fact that Job had also suffered *social* downfall,
of which we hear more in chapter 30.   But Job regards God
as the real author of it all.   The first part of verse 12 continues
the figure of the wild beast.   In the second half of 12, and in
13, it changes to a picture of God as the commander of a body
of archers.   In 14, the figure becomes that of warriors attacking a city and making breach upon breach in the walls.   In 14
GIANT should be 'warrior', and in verse 16 FOUL should be
translated 'inflamed'.

In verses 18 to end, it is plain that in his innermost heart
Job believes in God's fundamental righteousness, despite the
bold metaphors on his lips.   The plea here is not for vengeance
on his tormentor (compare the blood of Abel crying for
vengeance on Cain, Genesis 4.10), but for the vindication
by God of God's own righteousness.   This appeal is midway
between the cry of the blood of Abel for vengeance on wrong
committed, and the blood of our Lord, which speaks of God's
forgiveness of sin committed (see Heb. 12.24).   It reflects as
much a division in the mind of Job as a division in his conception of God.   In verse 21, we must follow the R.V.:

That He would maintain the right of a man with God,
And of a son of man with his neighbour.

Chapter 17

In verse 1 instead of MY BREATH IS CORRUPT we should
follow the R.V.:

My spirit is consumed.

DOTH NOT MINE EYE CONTINUE IN THEIR PROVOCATION? in verse 2

means: 'My soul is continually provoked by them.' In verse 3 Job is in effect asking God to accept arbitration before himself. STRIKE HANDS WITH ME means 'accept my pledge'. Verse 4 refers to the friends' insensitiveness. We must confess that verse 5 is hopelessly obscure in the Hebrew; A.V. and R.V. are equally distant from the original sense. Job seems to be criticising some aspect of his friends' position. In verse 6 the reference to Job's resemblance to a TABRET is absurd. We may read:

> And I am become as one at whom men spit.

The similarity with the Suffering Servant is strong; cf. Isaiah 50.6, Psalm 44.14. It seems impossible to force verses 8 and 9 to make sense in their context; at least it can only be done by ignoring every rule of probability. They directly contradict all that Job has been saying, and proceeds to say. We must treat them either as an insertion into the original text by some orthodox copyist who was shocked at Job's audacity, or as part of Bildad's speech in chapter eighteen, which has been included by a copyist's error in Job's speech. We shall find other places where verses have been displaced from their original position. We are in trouble with the text once more in verse 12. It seems a strange way of expressing the view that the friends' ideas are wrong. A reasonable guess is to translate the verse as if Job was quoting his friends:

> He (God) will change night into day,
> And the light is near unto darkness.

Job is protesting at the friends' easy optimism about his condition. Verses 13 to 15 will then be Job's answer to the friends' sanguine suggestions, and we must put an 'if' in front of each clause:

> If I must look to the grave as my house,
>   And make my bed in the darkness.
> If I say to corruption: Thou art my father,
>   To the worm: Thou art my mother and my sister,
> Then where is my hope? etc.

The sense of the verse is: if I indulge these hopes you speak of, the utmost I can expect is the grave. In verse 16, instead of BARS we must read 'together', and the sense becomes:

> Will they descend with me to She'ol?
> Shall we go down together to the pit?

As we study a chapter like this one, we must surely carry away two impressions. One is the absurdity of supposing that there can be anything like verbal infallibility in the Bible, when in such places as this it is so uncertain what the original words of the Bible were. The other is the providence of God, who has brought down even to our day the essential witness to His self-revelation through prophets and thinkers and supremely in Christ, despite all the finitude and fallibility of human records. Indeed, through all the obscurities of this chapter, something of God's self-revelation does shine. Job's appeal to God to be his surety reinforces the appeal of his blood mentioned in 16.18 to that God who he knows in his heart of hearts will listen. Compare Hebrews 7.22, where Jesus is described as the surety of that New Covenant which God has sworn to give. Job here is striving to vindicate that essentially Hebrew conception of the personal God, who makes promises to individuals, who calls them and uses them for His purposes. This conception is somewhat in contrast to the God of Job's friends, the God of conventional piety. The ways of that benevolent but not very enterprising autocrat are far from inscrutable, since they can be summed up in the simple formula: 'Good for the good and bad for the bad.'

Chapter 18   Bildad's Second Speech

There is a certain type of rule-of-thumb piety which is chiefly distinguished by harshness and even brutality toward those who do not observe its rules. The essence of this type of piety is self-righteousness and complacency; it has no room for faith in any sense but that of intellectual assent to the orthodox formula. It is this type of piety which Bildad exhibits. Every one of Bildad's sentences is a separate reflec-

tion on Job, and the whole constitutes a very hard and conventional exposition of the view which all the friends were concerned to defend. He begins by dismissing Job's profound and
intense searching for the personal God with the phrase ' snares
for words '. For other instances of this type of piety compare
the attitude of those who brought to our Lord the woman
taken in adultery (John 8.1-6), and Mr. Collins' judgement
on Lydia (*Pride and Prejudice*) uttered from the height of
moral superiority.

HOW LONG WILL YE MAKE AN END OF WORDS, verse 2, should
be translated as in the R.V.:

> How long will ye lay snares for words?

In view of what we have noted on 16.9 we must translate
verse 4 as:

> Thou that tearest thyself in thy anger (R.V.).

It is not God that tears Himself in rage, says Bildad, but Job.
The meaning of the rest of the verse is that Job can hardly
expect God to change His changeless decree that sin brings
punishment. It is as fixed as the laws of nature. For TO HIS
FEET in verse 11 we must read ' at his heels ' (R.V.). The first
half of verse 13 is probably wrong in the A.V. Moffatt translates it in this way:

> Sickness gnaws at his skin.

THE FIRST-BORN OF DEATH is probably a deadly disease. Translate the first half of verse 14 as follows:

> He shall be rooted out of the tent wherein he trusted.

THE KING OF TERRORS is a fine phrase for death. (But some
scholars suggest that this phrase and also 'the first-born of
death' are names for demons popularly supposed to afflict
mankind.) The first half of verse 15 must run:

> There shall dwell in his tent that which is none of his.

In verse 17 there is a contrast between EARTH and STREET (which
latter ought to be read as 'open steppe '). His name will be
rooted out both from the cultivated countryside and the open

steppe-land. SON NOR NEPHEW in verse 19 is a jingling phrase:
'chit nor child' is a good equivalent. THEY THAT COME AFTER
and THEY THAT WENT BEFORE in verse 20 seems to imply that
not only his successors, but those who died before him would
hear in She'ol of his fate and be appalled, which seems to
carry the idea to absurdity. The two phrases can just as well
be translated:

> They of the east . . . they of the west . . .

which gives better sense.

Chapter 19   Job's Response to Bildad's Second Speech

The sufferings of which Job complains are paralleled both
by those of the Suffering Servant (Isaiah 53) and by those of
our Lord. But in each case they are interpreted in a different
way. The Suffering Servant voluntarily accepts his sufferings
as a means of redemption for others; our Lord sees them as
God's will for Him, but there is no suggestion that He thought
of them as inflicted by God. In fact the key to the difference
between these various modes of understanding suffering lies
in the relation of the sufferer to God. Job understands his
own fundamental need of encounter with God, for the chapter
ends with a plea for meeting. Once more the problem of
innocent suffering, that seems at first sight the central problem
of the Book, passes over into the problem of man's relation to
God.

In verse 3 we must follow the R.V. and change MAKE YOUR-
SELVES STRANGE TO ME into:

> deal hardly with me.

BEHOLD, I CRY OUT OF WRONG is incorrect (v. 7). The A.V.
margin is right:

> Behold, I cry, Violence!

In verse 10 DESTROYED ME ON EVERY SIDE gives us the picture
of a building being pulled down. The reference in verse 17
to THE CHILDREN'S SAKE OF MY OWN BODY is not rightly translated. It does not mean his own children, but the children

who came from the same womb as himself.   It should be
read as follows:

I am loathsome to my own brethren.

In verse 20 a familiar proverb is to be found: I AM ESCAPED
WITH THE SKIN OF MY TEETH.   But the Hebrew from which
it is taken does not make good sense.   It can be emended to
run:

I am escaped with my skin in my teeth,

i.e. I have escaped with my life and nothing more.

Verses 25 to 29 present one of the most obscure passages
in the Book, as the Hebrew text has been very badly preserved.
Unfortunately it is a very important passage.   Both the A.V.
and the R.V. translations are bedevilled by a more or less
explicit intention to read into the passage a belief in the resurrection of the body (A.V. chapter heading· 'he believeth in
the resurrection').   This belief is not in fact to be found in
these verses.   As a recent scholar points out, if it were, it
would make the rest of the discussion unnecessary.   In verse
25 MY REDEEMER should be 'my vindicator' (R.V. margin); it
refers to God, and is the supreme example of Job appealing
from God to God.   In the second half of the verse we should
perhaps translate:

and that hereafter he will stand up upon the dust,

but whether 'dust' refers simply to the earth or to Job's grave
is not clear.   Verse 26 is hopelessly corrupt, and it is really
impossible to guess what the original words were.   WORMS
seems to be an invention of the A.V. translators; they are not
to be found in the Hebrew, corrupt though it is.   The only
part of the verse that even faintly approaches clarity in the
Hebrew is: I SHALL SEE GOD.   Job possibly did expect to see
God when the time of his vindication should come, though we
cannot say whether this was to be before or after his death.
In verse 27 AND NOT ANOTHER is certainly incorrect.   The
Hebrew means 'a stranger'.   We may probably trace in this

the affirmation that when Job's vindication shall come he shall find God no longer estranged. The meaning of the second half of the verse seems lost beyond recall. Verse 28 is so obscure as to defy even guess work. It may contain a reference to the friends' hostility. The only part of verse 29 that we can decipher with any reasonable probability is BE YE AFRAID OF THE SWORD. Job is warning his friends to beware of God's judgement on their lack of sympathy.

Fortunately there is one important thing that does stand out of this appallingly confused passage: Job still hopes somehow (whether in the body or out of the body, we know not) for vindication before God. But it is a pity that we cannot be sure whether this encounter is to be before or after death. The author may have allowed the possibility of some sort of life after death to pass across his mind. That is as much as we can say.

Chapter 20   Zophar's Second Speech

Zophar says nothing to advance the argument. He merely gives a highly embellished account of the dreadful fate of the wicked in this life. Like Eliphaz in 4.12-17, he too produces a 'spiritual experience' to enforce his argument (v. 3), but it is no more convincing than Eliphaz's. The picture that he draws of the wicked man is that of a greedy, grasping, and ruthless social oppressor.

The A.V. in verse 2 is not satisfactory; a better guess is:

> To calm my anxious thoughts that disturb me,
> And because of my agitation within me. . . .

This leads naturally on to verse 3: I HAVE HEARD THE CHECK OF MY REPROACH which should be read as follows:

> And out of my understanding a spirit answereth me.

The meaning is a little like Milton's sonnet:

> Doth God exact day labour, light denied?
> I fondly ask. But Patience to prevent
> That murmur soon replies. . . .

That is, when the poet's mind is agitated by the apparent anomaly in God's ways, God's spirit within him (as he believes) reproaches his impatience, and explains that the wicked will soon be punished. In verse 11 we must follow the R.V.:

> His bones are full of his youth
> But it shall lie down with him in the dust.

The wicked shall meet with premature death. In verses 12 to 14 the sin of the wicked is compared to some delightful sweetmeat which is kept long in the mouth, but when it is eventually swallowed proves to be deadly poison.

A good emendation of the first half of verse 17 is:

> He shall not see the rivers of oil.

Take the second half of 21 as

> therefore his prosperity shall not endure (R.V).

Similarly the second half of 22 should probably be:

> Everyone that is in misery shall come upon him.

The words WHEN HE IS ABOUT TO FILL HIS BELLY in verse 23 are very doubtful. It is better to omit them. The meaning of verse 24 is: 'Though the spear may miss, the arrow will strike'; for IT IS DRAWN AND COMETH OUT OF THE BODY in verse 25, we should read the R.V.'s

> He draweth it forth.

In default of new arguments, Zophar seems determined to make Job's flesh creep!

III

THIRD CYCLE OF SPEECHES
Chapters 21 to 31

Chapter 21 **Job's Response to Zophar's Second Speech**
In this chapter Job refutes vigorously the contention of the
friends that the wicked are invariably punished, or that their
day is brief, or that their children suffer. And he rebukes the
friends for offering him a false picture of God's ways. He
prefers the truth, even though it leaves him face to face with
an inscrutable mystery.

In verse 4 Job means that his complaint is not to man, but
about God. Job expresses astonishment in verses 5 and 6 at
the appalling fact that God actually favours the wicked. He
then answers Zophar's detailed description of the punishment
of the ungodly by a detailed description of the prosperity of
the ungodly. ORGAN in verse 12 is an anachronism for which
the A.V. is responsible: 'Pipe' (R.V.) is correct. In verses
16 to 30 there occur at intervals words which are directly
opposed to all that Job has been saying up to this (e.g. 16, 18,
19, 20, 30). To allow them to stand as Job's real sentiments
would be to convict our author of utter inconsistency. We
must either emend them, treat them as quotations from the
friends' speeches made by Job in order to refute them, or
attribute them to a later copyist who wished to modify Job's
shocking utterances. A good example occurs in verse 16:
first clause here is well rendered by Moffatt as:

Are they not masters of their fortune?

But the second half, THE COUNSEL OF THE WICKED IS FAR FROM
ME sounds very much like the pious statement of a later copyist replacing perhaps a lost line.   Verse 17 can be retained
more or less as it stands in the A.V., except that we must
make all three clauses into indignant questions.   This will
mean inserting ' How often does God . . . ? at the beginning
of the third clause.   The answer expected is of course:
' Never! '   The same process must be applied to verse 18:
' How often is it that they are stubble . . .' etc.   The friends'
argument will then be quoted in the first half of 19, and Job's
reply to it come in the second half of the verse and in verse 20,
thus:

> You say: God layeth up iniquity for his children.
>   I reply: Let God recompense the wicked man himself,
>   that he may know it.
> Let his own eyes see his destruction,
>   And let him drink of the wrath of the Almighty.

Verse 21 pursues the same line of thought.   We must translate:

> What does it matter to him what happens to his house after
>   him,
> When the number of his months is finished?

Job is meeting the friends' contention that the wicked is
punished in his children.   Job's argument is a sound one, and
applies just as forcibly to the Utopianism of the modern Communist.   The Communist urges the workers to sacrifice themselves for a future happy condition which will only benefit
their posterity.   We should probably attribute verse 22 to
some later copyist.   It does not fit the context, and can hardly
be another quotation from the friends.

In verses 23 to 26, Job is complaining not that God rules
the world unjustly, but that it does not seem to run on any
principles at all.   In verse 24 HIS BREASTS ARE FULL OF MILK
ought probably to be translated as

> His thighs are full of fat.

In verses 28 to 30, Job is once more quoting the friends in order to refute them, though the A.V. text makes this anything but clear. WHERE IS THE HOUSE . . . WHERE ARE THE DWELLING PLACES, etc., in verse 28, is the friends' argument, and means: 'They are gone, destroyed by God.' Job answers in verse 29: 'Ask the man in the street, he will tell you that the evidence is unmistakable.' The evidence is given in verse 30 and it is to the effect that the wicked pass unscathed through all disasters. But to get this sense from verse 30 the A.V. translation must be modified thus:

> That the wicked is preserved in the day of destruction;
> They shall be rescued from the day of wrath.

It is quite possible that a later copyist made the slight alteration in the Hebrew, which is all that is necessary to reverse this sense. By making the small alteration he gave the orthodox view, regardless of the fact that it made nonsense in the context. In verses 31 to 33 Job insists that, far from being forgotten after death, as the friends have suggested (18.17; 20.7), the ungodly has 'a lovely funeral', and even, if the Hebrew of verses 32 to 33 can be trusted, seems to derive some sort of gratification after death from the arrangements connected with his tomb—a doctrine which seems to be held by many to-day, judging by the elaborate memorials which are erected over the dead. AS THERE ARE INNUMERABLE BEFORE HIM, verse 33, is very doubtful. This verse, together with verse 32 may contain a description of the splendid funeral cortège, with a long line of mourners in front and behind.

We have noticed the activity of pious scribes in this chapter, and will have occasion to do so again. We may deplore it, but it may be that this injection of pious sentiments was responsible for the preservation of the Book till it had secured its place among the sacred books. Had Job's meaning been plain to all, it might never have been handed down to posterity. The final verse of this chapter contains a salutary reminder of the necessity for dealing honestly with honest doubt. The honest man cannot find comfort in wishful thinking or arguments based on part of the evidence only.

Chapter 22   **Eliphaz's Third Speech**

Eliphaz's argument runs like this: if you are righteous, it is in your own interest to be so, not God's.   God automatically gives good to the good and evil to the wicked; therefore, as you are receiving evil, you are wicked.   Therefore be good, that you may receive good.

In verse 4 we must follow the R.V. translation:

Is it for thy fear of him that he reproveth thee?

i.e. 'you're not going to be so absurd as to suggest that he punishes you for your piety, therefore it must be for your sin.' In verses 6 to 9 Eliphaz accuses Job of committing a whole catalogue of crimes, which he draws out of his imagination. This provides an interesting sidelight on the nature of conventional piety.   Here we have one of its great characteristics exemplified, the tendency to accuse those who sin against it not only of heresy, but of every other imaginable vice.   In the early Church we find it in the habit which soon grew up of not only condemning a heretic for his own errors of doctrine, but of branding him also as 'atheist', 'Judas', and 'apostate'. Even so great a Christian as St. Bernard in his prosecution of Abelard, could not restrain himself from accusing him indiscriminately of every heresy under the sun.   Nearer our own times, we find in John Wesley's journal instances of similar treatment meted out to him by Church of England clergy outraged by his unconventional methods.[1]   This tendency is not confined to Christian believers, as one can see from the vituperative epithets 'Fascist', 'cannibal', etc., that pious Communists hurl at 'deviationists'.

Verse 8 makes no sense in the context; we may omit it as a

[1] NOTE: A good modern instance occurred when Hensley Henson was appointed Bishop of Hereford in 1918. 'The Church Union' suggested that its members should use the Collect for St. Matthias Day, thereby implying that Hensley Henson was another Judas.

later footnote explaining the doctrine Eliphaz is refuting, or we might conclude that it has got displaced, and originally came after verse 14, where Eliphaz is in fact quoting Job's words to refute them. The meaning of verse 14 is: 'You say that God does not concern Himself with man's affairs.' We find Eliphaz's answer to this argument in verses 15 and 16: it is the well-worn answer that the wicked do eventually come to a dreadful end. We must follow the R.V. in verse 17:

> What can the Almighty do for us?

Verse 18 is a problem: the second half bears all the marks of the shocked editor (cf. 21.16). The first half is better omitted altogether. Verse 20 is incorrect in the A.V. A good guess is:

> Surely their substance is cut off,
> And their abundance the fire consumeth.

In verse 21 THEREBY GOOD SHALL COME UNTO THEE is impossible. The word translated SHALL COME must be taken as 'income'. Moffatt renders well:

> It will mean prosperity for you.

In verse 24, we have not really got a promise of wealth (which is contained perhaps in the next verse), but an injunction to abandon wealth:

> And lay thou thy treasure in the dust,
> And the gold of Ophir among the stones of the brook.

Bold guesses are needed in verse 29; here is a fair one:

> For he abaseth one that speaketh proudly,
> But the lowly of eyes he saveth.

The ISLAND of verse 30 is a romantic invention apparently of the A.V. translators. This seems to be the sense:

> So he doth rescue an innocent man,
> And he is delivered by the cleanness of his hands.

Chapters 23 and 24   **Job's Response to Eliphaz's Third Speech**
(Except 24.18 to 20: see note at this point)

From here until the end of chapter 30 we enter upon a toss-
ing sea of doubts about the original meaning of the Hebrew
text. The original Hebrew of these chapters must have been
seriously damaged at one time. We must just set our teeth
and do our best to appreciate the material of real value which
does appear through the mists. Fortunately chapter 28 forms
a patch of still water in the middle of the storm.

Chapter 23
The debate on the problem of the prosperity of the wicked
leads Job to the profounder question of his own relationship
to God. The prosperity of the wicked, he insists, is a fact, and
the understanding of that fact lies in attaining the right
relationship to God, a relationship which he does not yet
possess. Part of his misery is that he feels himself at the
moment to be the target of God's hostility, though he is conscious that there is something deeper than that, and that God
is a moral God. Yet when he wishes for this deeper relationship, he lacks the technique for finding God. In this he differs
from the friends, who thought that they knew exactly what
God was like and what He was doing. This conviction that
he can do nothing of himself to find God shows the author of
Job's profound unity with the deepest thought of the O.T.
The prophets know no technique for finding God, their God is
a God who calls them and reveals Himself. Unlike Plato, who
taught that man can find God by reason, or Hindu seers who
recommend certain disciplines for finding Him, the O.T.
prophets and N.T. writers know only a God who reveals Himself when it is His pleasure to do so, and is yet not a capricious
despot, but a righteous ruler of His world. In the Bible the
devotee does not search for God, he waits for God; cf. Isaiah
45.15, 'Verily thou art a God that hidest thyself', and Luke
2.25 and 38, 'Waiting for the consolation of Israel.'
In verse 2 'rebellious' is better than BITTER. Job does not

feel at all like giving in. We should translate the second half
of the verse as:

His hand is heavy upon my groaning.

i.e. I groan, but he afflicts me all the heavier for that. The
second half of verse 6 should run:

but he would give heed unto me (R.V.).

Instead of I SHOULD BE DELIVERED FROM MY JUDGE in verse 7
we should probably read:

I should win my suit.

ON THE LEFT HAND, WHERE HE DOTH WORK is not a satisfactory
translation of verse 9. It should be changed to:

I seek him on the left hand.

Probably what Job is saying in verse 10 is: 'But if he knew
the way that I take, I would come forth from the trial like
gold.' If God would give him a fair trial, he would certainly
be acquitted. DECLINED in verse 11 means 'deviated'. Translate the second half of verse 12 as:

I have treasured up the words of his mouth in my bosom.

HE IS IN ONE MIND in verse 13 is a guess by the translators, for
the word MIND is not in the Hebrew. We should emend it to

He has chosen,

i.e. He has arbitrarily fixed my destiny of suffering. In verse 14
MANY SUCH THINGS ARE WITH HIM, if it means anything, means
that this is the way He always behaves. The R.V. rendering
'faint' in verse 16 is better than the A.V. SOFT. Verse 17 is
very obscure: perhaps Job is cursing his day again, or perhaps
complaining that God has forgotten him.

In parts of this chapter (e.g. verses 13 to 17) it is God's
inscrutability that overwhelms Job, not the feeling that God is
fundamentally unjust. He is quite unable to fathom God's
dealings with him and cannot grasp the nature of the relationship between God and himself. Job feels that the moral law
which he has striven to keep is God's law, and never, for all

his bewilderment, seriously suggests that God and His law
have parted company.

Chapter 24

In this chapter Job elaborates his theme that God lets the
unrighteous prosper and the righteous suffer. He goes into
details and gives a vivid picture of unjust social conditions.
It reminds one of the graphic descriptions of social conditions
in the prophets, but it is without the fire of their indignation.
It has a note of despair in it. Indeed, as Job reviews the
evidence (his own uprightness, his calamities, the sufferings of
other people, the triumph of the wicked) he even contemplates
the possibility of an unjust God. This state of doubt was a
necessary prelude to the revelation God makes in chapter 38.
Often in the new revelations which God makes of His nature
there seems at first sight to be a complete inversion of conventional ideas. The supreme example of this comes in the
Cross: Our Lord is the King of Glory, but to those who passed
by the Cross, He must have seemed more aptly called Lord
of Shame; cf. I Cor. 1.18-28.

We must follow the R.V. in the first half of verse 1:

Why are times not laid up by the Almighty?

The times Job looks for are judgement-days, when God would
decisively intervene in favour of the righteous. This question
'Why doesn't God intervene?' is one which, besides being
echoed all through the O.T., is actually repeated in mockery
by the Jewish authorities and those who passed by, as our
Lord hung on the Cross. The astonishing thing is that God
was intervening in the most decisive manner at the very
moment when Jesus was being mocked; cf. Mark 15.29-32.
In verse 5 the comparison seems to be between the poor, who
have to seek their daily food, and the wild ass who has to seek
his, unlike the domestic ass, who has it provided for him.
Instead of RISING BETIMES FOR A PREY translate:

They labour for their food.

THEY in this verse refers to the poor of the earth, as in verse 4, second part. THEY are also the subject in verse 6. In that verse CORN is a bad translation. The word means 'mixed fodder for cattle'. The sense is probably that the poor have to eat food only fit for cattle. Similarly the VINTAGE means literally 'late gleanings', all that is left for the poor to take. The poor are still the subject in verse 7, the first clause of which should read:

> They lie all night naked without clothing.

They continue to be the subject in verse 8. In verse 9 the subject changes to the oppressors of the poor. In verses 10 and 11 we are back again at a description of the poor. Thus verse 10 must be translated as in the R.V.:

> They go about naked without clothing,
> And being hungry they carry the sheaves.

In verse 11 WITHIN THEIR WALLS should probably be 'between the rows of olives'. In the midst of the wealth belonging to the rich the poor are in want. The subject changes so much in this passage from poor to rich and back again, without any indication of change of subject in the Hebrew, that many scholars try to tidy it up. It actually stands thus: THEY means 'oppressors' in verse 3 and the first part of verse 4; 'the poor' in the second part of verse 4 to verse 8; 'oppressors' in verse 9; 'the poor' in verses 10 and 11. One suggestion is that verse 9 originally stood after the first half of verse 4, or after verse 12. Verse 12 seems to indicate a transition from country wrongs to city wrongs. The following verses describe the sins of the townsman. We gain the impression in this chapter that our author is recording his own observations in a very direct way. He was a much more profound commentator on the social scene than some of those who were probably his near-contemporaries, e.g. the author of the book of Malachi, or Nehemiah. Verse 12 itself needs some emendation. The following is an improvement on the A.V.:

> From out of the populous city men groan,
> And the soul of the wounded crieth out:
> Yet God heareth not their prayer.

LIGHT in verse 13 probably has no moral connotation. The meaning is simply: 'there are night-walkers'. Some retranslation and rearrangement is needed in verses 14 to 17. The following is probably as near the original as we can hope to get:

> The murderer riseth in the dark:
> He killeth the poor and needy.
> The eye of the adulterer waiteth for the twilight,
> Saying, No eye shall see me,
> And he disguiseth his face.
> In the night the chief goeth about,
> In the dark they dig through houses;
> They shut themselves up in the daytime,
> They know not the light.
> For the morning is to all of them as the shadow of death,
> For they know its terrors.

Notice that in this chapter Job is primarily concerned to point out that the wicked commit these crimes and go unpunished, not that it is the righteous that suffer them. There are some parts of India to-day where this description is directly applicable. Incidentally orthodox Hinduism justifies the sufferings of the under-privileged on much the same grounds as the friends do, except that it brings in reincarnation as a palliative.

In so far as any meaning can be extracted from the wreck of the original text of verses 18 to 20, they seem to express sentiments exactly opposed to all that Job has been saying so far. It is best to assume that they have strayed from Bildad's speech in chapter 25, which is obviously mutilated. The first part of verse 18 refers to God's coming with floods to overwhelm the wicked. The second half is meaningless in the A.V. Moffatt's guess is a good one:

> No foot turns to his (the wicked man's) vineyard.

The translation of verse 19 is very doubtful, but no satisfactory alternative can be suggested. Likewise all that can be said of verse 20 is that it expresses the sentiment that the memory

of the wicked is short-lived. There is so much doubt about
the original meaning of verses 21 to 25 that commentators have
understood them in directly opposite senses, but on the whole
verse 24 seems to belong to Bildad's speech describing the
horrid fate of the wicked, and the other verses to Job's speech
describing their abuse of power and their prosperity. We can
fairly confidently translate verse 22 as:

> Yet God by his power maketh the mighty to continue:

> He (the mighty) riseth up though he believed not that he
> would live.

Verse 23 is hopelessly uncertain; the second half could mean
either that God marks him to punish him or to bless him.
Instead of THEY ARE TAKEN OUT OF THE WAY LIKE ALL OTHERS
read:

> They are plucked off like mallows.

The sense fits Bildad's speech much better than Job's.

Chapter 25   A Fragment of Bildad's Third Speech

This chapter we may certainly take as only a fragment of
Bildad's original speech. Some scholars have suggested that
its very shortness is a subtle way of indicating that the friends'
arguments are exhausted. But this seems unlikely. As a
matter of fact, when we examine chapters 26 and 27, we find
that most of them are much more appropriate in the mouth
of the friends than in Job's. So it seems likely that we have
in chapters 25 to 27 three separate blocks of speeches belonging to the friends, with a small fragment of a speech of Job's.
Chapter 25 all belongs to Bildad. Chapter 26 all belongs to
one of the friends, Bildad or Zophar (to whom a third speech
is not assigned in our present text); 27.1-6 belongs to Job;
and 27.7-23 belongs to one of the friends (Bildad or Zophar).

In verse 3 for HIS LIGHT ARISE we should follow a better
translation and read: 'his ambush spring.' In verse 6 a good
translation is:

> How much less man that is a maggot?

Chapter 26 **Another Fragment of a Speech of Bildad or Zophar**

The ingenuity of many commentators has been exercised in explaining how this chapter can possibly be made consistent with Job's other sentiments. It is far more satisfactory to take it either as the speech of Bildad or of Zophar.

If these conclusions about this chapter are right, verse 1 must be looked on as an explanatory comment by a later copyist, who either found the text already in confusion, or wished to attribute *some* pious sentiments to Job. Verses 2 and 3 mean: 'You haven't done much to help the man whose faith in God is shaken by observing the injustice in the world.' Moffatt's lively translation is:

> What a help you are to poor God!
> What a support to His failing powers!

Verse 4 means: 'Are you speaking like this to God, speaking by His inspiration? What an absurd idea!' The A.V. is misleading in verse 5; we should read:

> The Rephaim tremble under the waters,
> The inhabitants of She'ol quake.

The Rephaim are the shades in She'ol. She'ol was thought of as under the earth, but the earth itself was conceived of as floating in water, so She'ol was under water. The NORTH in verse 7 means the top of the dome of heaven. This heaven is not, apparently, supported by anything in the middle, so it can be described as hanging upon nothing. We must understand EARTH here to include the whole firmament. Read in verse 9 for HOLDETH BACK the words 'closeth in'. His throne is on the top of the dome, but He hides it in clouds. In verse 10 translate the first clause as:

> He hath marked out a circle on the face of the waters.

The earth is thought of as a hemisphere; God has placed this circular earth on the waters. Where the earth ends is where the light passes into darkness. THE PILLARS OF HEAVEN in verse 11 means the mountains situated along the edge of the earth, which serve to hold up the inverted bowl of the sky. The PROUD in verse 12 conceals a reference to the chaos-monster. We should translate the words as 'Rahab'. In verse 13 GARNISHED is not quite correct: 'cleared' is better. His wind clears the heavens of clouds. The second half of the verse contains another reference to Tiamat-Rahab. For CROOKED we should read 'fleeing'. God put the monster to flight, and thus brought order out of chaos: cf. Isaiah, chapter 27.

Chapters 27, verses 1 to 6   **A Fragment from a Reply of Job**

Only the first six verses of this chapter can belong to Job: the rest breathe the sentiments of the friends. These six verses would go well before chapter 29, as a preface to Job's final protestation of innocence, and may well have originally stood there. For Job there are only three fixed points in his perplexity: the wrongness of the conventional account of God's government of the world, his own innocence, the belief that somewhere, somehow, a just God would vindicate him. Within these limits Job's thoughts wander; now he accuses God of injustice, now he asserts his belief that God would justify him, now he protests that God has refused him judgement, now he says that he will never abandon his plea. The argument in the Book of Job does not proceed by logical steps from point to point.

In verse 1 the phrase CONTINUED HIS PARABLE AND SAID is a new introductory formula, and probably betrays the hand of the man who re-arranged the material in these chapters; cf. chapter 29. Notice in verse 2 that Job still swears by the God whose integrity he denounces. The sense of verse 3 is, apparently: 'While I still have any strength, I will use it in protesting my innocence.' THAT I SHOULD JUSTIFY YOU in verse 5 means:

That I should accept your account of things.

Chapter 27, verses 7 to 23   **A Third Fragment of a Speech of Bildad or Zophar**

In this fragment absolutely nothing is added to what the friends have already said.

In verse 8, instead of THOUGH HE HATH GAINED we should read:

> When he is cut off.

Also TAKETH AWAY HIS SOUL is better translated 'requireth his soul', cf. Luke 12.20. The HYPOCRITE is 'the ungodly'. We must follow the R.V. in verse 11:

> I will teach you concerning the hand of God,

i.e. how His government works. HIS WIDOWS SHALL NOT WEEP in verse 15 means that there will be no formal funeral with the widow weeping as convention demanded. The plural may refer to the polygamy of patriarchal times. A BOOTH in verse 18 is the temporary shelter put up in harvest time for the man or woman who is set to watch the crops. In verse 19 it is better on the whole to make HE SHALL NOT BE GATHERED and HE IS NOT refer to the riches, not the rich man. He lies down one night a wealthy man; no human hand takes his wealth away, but when he awakes in the morning it has vanished by an act of divine judgement.

First Interpolation

Chapter 28   **In Praise of Wisdom**

Virtually all modern scholars agree that this chapter has no real connection with what precedes or follows it. It is quite unsuitable for Job to utter in his exasperated frame of mind, and is too calm and reflective for the friends. Also, there is some evidence that the Hebrew is different from what our author uses. It seems to be an independent poem, of great beauty, inserted in the text by some later poet. If we regard it as an insertion, we may welcome it as an *entr'acte*; it makes something of a pause in the action of the poem. The friends

have had their last say. Job is about to make his final speech
for the defence. We pause for a moment to consider the
essential inscrutability of God (which is after all a leading
theme in the poem) before we descend once more into the
strong emotional situation of Job. The main purport of the
poem, expressed in glorious language, is: 'Intellectual specula-
tions about God are useless: follow the rule of simple piety.'
Compare Psalm 131 and I Timothy 6.20-21 (a passage probably
written after St. Paul's day.)

Most of the poem consists of what might be called an ode
on man's great achievements. Probably within a hundred years
or so of these verses being written, another poet, this time
a Greek, wrote in very much the same strain. 'Many are the
wonders of the world,' says Sophocles, 'but none is more
wonderful than man.' As our Hebrew poet looks at man's
works he realizes that beyond all of them stands the wisdom
of God, to which man would do well to turn. The Greek poet
does not think of God in this connection, but only of the
tragedy of this wonderful creature continually frustrated by his
own passions. European literature since the first World War
has driven home to us the sentiments of the Greek poet *ad
nauseam*. But the Hebrew poet's conclusion is surely more
relevant to our day.

In verse 3 SEARCHETH OUT ALL PERFECTION should rather be:

Searcheth out to the furthest bound (R.V.).

The verse refers to man's taking with him his own lights into
the mine where he works. SHADOW OF DEATH in the A.V. is
very often (as here) a mistranslation for 'thick darkness'.
Translate the first line of verse 4 as:

He breaketh open a shaft away from where men sojourn
  (R.V.).

In ancient times copper-mining was carried on in the Sinaitic
peninsula, one of the most desolate places in the world; compare modern oil-wells in Arabia. The second half of the

verse seems to portray the diversion of underground streams met with in the course of operations. We might translate:

The waters diminish, they are diverted by man.

In verse 5, instead of TURNED UP AS IT WERE FIRE read:

hollowed out by fire;

the poet is describing the process of lighting fires under boulders to render them more brittle to the pickaxe, and he contrasts the creative activities of the farmer on the surface with the destructive operations of the miner under the earth. The R.V. of verse 7 makes the meaning clear:

That path no bird of prey knoweth,
Neither hath the falcon's eye seen it.

For RIVERS in verse 10 read 'passages' (R.V.); it is probably a reference to the galleries of a mine. The sense in verse 11 seems good but the Hebrew is a little strange, so some scholars alter the Hebrew slightly and translate:

He searcheth the beds of rivers.

This would describe the process of panning for gold. CRYSTAL in verse 17 really means 'glass' (R.V.), which was much more valuable in ancient times than it is to-day. In verses 21 and 22, the inhabitants of the three divisions of the created universe, earth, air, and She'ol, deny that they contain the dwelling-place of Wisdom. TO MAKE THE WEIGHT FOR THE WINDS in verse 25 means that he decreed the velocity of the wind, and set a limit to its speed.

In verses 25 and 26, Wisdom is associated with the Creation; cf. Proverbs 8.22ff. This perhaps dates the poem as belonging to the Greek Period (333-165 B.C.). During that period Hebrew thinkers were led to emphasize the thought of the Divine Wisdom almost as if it were a separate and peculiar part of God's nature. They saw this Wisdom as specially manifested in the creation of the world. This emphasis on the Wisdom of God was no doubt an answer to the great principle of Greek philosophy, the Word, or Logos. Greek philosophy was be-

coming increasingly popular in Israel, and the Jewish scholars
felt that they must show that their own religion could supply
all that Greek philosophy offered. The author of the Fourth
Gospel boldly claims the title of 'the Word of God' for Jesus
Christ (John 1.1-18). In this chapter of Job the poet is certainly introducing the thought of the Divine Wisdom as the
underlying principle of the universe, but he does not much
emphasize its connection with the Creation.

Chapters 29 to 31   Job's Final Challenge

In these three chapters we find Job's former condition
represented as being that of the typical Old Testament saint,
that is, a rich and influential man like Abraham, ruling over
his possessions with wisdom and mercy. But in chapter 31 a
far deeper type of piety is revealed, which is in fact a state of
the will rather than a series of good actions. One of the
objects of our author was to show that even this type of piety
is not sufficient.

Chapter 29

CONTINUED HIS PARABLE is an indication of the transpositions
which have taken place in the text. In the original there would
have been no need for this phrase. The friends are now silent,
and Job proceeds to his final self-vindication. In verse 4,
instead of the A.V.'s THE SECRET OF GOD WAS UPON MY TENT,
Moffatt's translation should be followed:

When God was kindly sheltering my home.

BUTTER and OIL in verse 6 are simply symbols of prosperity.
The second half of the verse means that even his stoniest
fields yielded olives. The YOUNG MEN hiding themselves in
verse 8 means that they withdrew in deference to his position.
In verse 14 'justice' (R.V.) is a better translation than JUDGE-
MENT. I SHALL DIE IN MY NEST (v. 18) is probably better translated:

I shall die with my nestlings around me.

In verse 20 Job says his bow was 'supple in my hand', rather than RENEWED. It describes his physical vigour, not his archery. The following translation of verse 24 should be used:

If I ridiculed a suggestion, all others refused to entertain it,
If I approved, they did not disapprove.

His reference to A KING IN THE ARMY in verse 25 must not be taken literally: it means that he had a kingly authority among his dependents.

Chapter 30

The description of the outcast folk in this chapter heightens the picture of the misery of Job. He is abandoned by God and scorned by the lowest of his fellow-men.

The meaning and relevance of verse 2 is obscure. Is Job saying that, bad as is the condition of these outcasts, his is worse? In the first part of verse 3, read 'gaunt' instead of SOLITARY. The rest of the verse must be more drastically changed:

Men who gnaw the dry ground,
Whose mother is devastation and desolation.

is a fair guess. In the end of verse 4 read:

juniper roots for their fuel.

BRAYED in verse 7 is curious; we could translate it as 'howled with lust', and WERE GATHERED TOGETHER would then mean 'mated'; i.e. 'they behave like beasts in their habits'. Not VILER THAN THE EARTH in verse 8, but 'outcasts from the land' (R.V. margin).

In verses 11 to 18 the Hebrew text is in a state of great confusion, and there are several places where we must just give up the struggle to recover the original text. It is complicated by the fact that very often we cannot be sure whether Job is speaking of 'He' (God) or 'they' (the outcast folk whom God allows to insult Him). In verse 11 LET LOOSE THE BRIDLE

BEFORE ME would mean that they do not try to hide their contempt. Moffatt's translation of verse 12 is good:

> A rabble rises against me,
> They set on me to besiege me.

In verse 13 THEY HAVE NO HELPER is wrong:

> there is none to restrain them

is perhaps the sense. WATERS in verse 14 is misleading; the figure is of a breach in the wall of a besieged city. In the second half of the verse it is Job who rolls:

> I am tossed about in the storm

is probably the sense. Verse 17 also must be changed to:

> By night my bones are corroded and fall away from me,
> And the pains that gnaw me lie not down to rest.

Reconstruction of verse 18 is hopeless; we can only surmise that it contains some description of his disease. For MY SUBSTANCE in verse 22 read with the R.V. 'in the storm'. What the Hebrew of verse 24 means, we simply cannot tell with any certainty. PREVENTED in verse 27 means 'are come upon me'. In verse 28 change I GO MOURNING WITHOUT THE SUN to

> I go mourning without comfort.

DRAGONS in verse 29 should be 'jackals'. The point of the comparison is the howl, not the strangeness. In verse 31 ORGAN must become 'pipe' (cf. 21.12).

Chapter 31

It is interesting to notice the legal phraseology in Job's approach to God that characterizes this chapter, e.g. verses 35 to 37. The author of the Book intends us to understand that Job, when he finally meets God face to face, realizes that his self-confident self-righteousness is not the right attitude to God. In this sense the Book of Job is the Epistle to the

Romans of the O.T. The author certainly got away from legalism; he understood what faith means, but not the astounding grace of God. He understood, however, much of the nature of God. The characteristics of the righteous man described in this chapter show that our author understood God's demand for an obedience springing from inner conviction and not a mere external fulfilment of a moral code. In fact this chapter can stand comparison with the Sermon on the Mount as given in St. Matthew's Gospel. Compare the following passages:

> Job 31.1 and 9: adultery of the eye; cf. Matt. 5.27-28.
> Job 31.29: hatred of enemies; cf. Matt. 5.21-22.
> Job 31.33: hypocrisy; cf. Matt. 7.5.
> Job 31.34: moral courage; cf. Matt. 5.11-12.

But all this only goes to show that it is quite possible for the most spiritual and inward type of piety to be intensely legalistic if unredeemed by a real encounter with the grace of God. It is because he realized this that the author of Job comes so near to the N.T.

In verse 3 for STRANGE PUNISHMENT read 'disaster' of the R.V. In the verses 5 and 6 we have the first of Job's asseverations by which he protests his innocence; each is followed by a terrible consequence which Job is willing to accept if he is wrong. We must not infer from these consequences that Job thought the ruin of his wife, death of his children, etc., would be a just retribution for his falsity; he is merely saying that if he is to be proved guilty then everything is topsy-turvy. In verse 10 GRIND UNTO seems to be a euphemism for 'be the concubine of '. Verse 11 is very probably a later comment by a pious scribe, who records his horror at such a shocking suggestion. Verse 12 may well be part of the same comment. In verses 13 and 14 we are reminded of our Lord's parable of the unmerciful servant (Matthew 18.23-35), but here it is expressed in terms of justice, there in terms of mercy.

Notice in verse 15 and the following verses the very humane views of Job on social relationships, which emphasize all the more the injustice of his fate. Indeed this extraordinarily high code of conduct is characteristic of this chapter. Another really astonishing feature of this chapter is the way. in which several of Jesus' parables are vividly evoked. With verses 17, 19 and 20 compare the Parable of the Sheep and the Goats (Matthew 25.31-46); see also the note on verses 13 and 14. Verses 24 and 25 recall the Parable of the Rich Fool (Luke 12.16-21.) If the Book of Job in the Old Testament could come so near to the standard of the Sermon on the Mount, and yet conclude that this is not enough, how essential it is to realize that the Pauline epistles must be read side by side with the gospels, Romans 7 with Matthew 5, if we are to understand the full significance of the work of Christ for us. In verse 18 we should read:

> For from my youth he brought me up like a father,
> And from my mother's womb did he guide me.

This gives us a specific reference to the fatherhood of God, and avoids the ludicrous notion of Job guiding the widow from his infancy. The meaning of verse 21 is that Job resisted the temptation to use his great position to sway the legal decision in his own favour. The first half of verse 28 is no doubt the pious scribe at work again, protesting against idolatry. The second half is the work of the original author but should be translated:

> And if I disowned God above . . .

Verse 31 must be changed; what the men of Job's house said was:

> Who can find one that hath not been satisfied with
>   hospitality?

AS ADAM in verse 33 is a possible translation, but ADAM in Hebrew means simply 'man' so we could translate it

> hide my transgression from men,

which is probably better. After verse 34 we must insert verses

38 to 40 which are much more suitable here as they express
the renunciation of one more sin.   Verses 35 to 37, the last
great protestation of integrity, make a fitting climax.   The
text in verses 35 to 37 is very uncertain: on the whole it
seems more likely that the BOOK of verse 35 is Job's protestation of innocence, not the adversary's accusation, which it is
hard to imagine Job as wearing with pride.   In the middle of
verse 35, instead of MY DESIRE IS THAT THE ALMIGHTY WOULD
ANSWER ME the Hebrew really gives the sense:

> Behold my Tau, let the Almighty answer me.

Tau is the last letter of the Hebrew alphabet, and was used as
a mark instead of a signature.   So the sense may be 'Here is
my signature; let God answer it.'   If we take the BOOK in this
verse as Job's protestation of integrity, we must translate the
second half of verse 35 as:

> Behold my Tau, let the Almighty answer me,
> And (let him answer) the scroll which his adversary (myself)
>   hath written.

It is, however, possible to take the BOOK as referring to God's
accusation (though this is less likely); with such a thought we
can compare 13.22 and 23.   On either interpretation it is clear
that these verses revert to that deeply significant element in
Job's thought, the appeal from God to God.   In the second
half of verse 37 instead of WOULD I GO NEAR, we should
follow the R.V. margin and read:

> would I present it (my protest) to him.

Job's meaning in verses 38 and 39 is that he has not acquired
his land unlawfully.

IV

SECOND INTERPOLATION: ELIHU'S SPEECH

Chapters 32 to 37

We saw in Section 1 of the Introduction that the speech of Elihu seems to be a later interpolation. There are two very strong reasons for this view, which may be summed up under the heads of *position* and *contents*. The Elihu speech comes as an anti-climax; the friends have already fallen silent; Job has made his last great protest. The stage is set for the appearance of God. Instead of that, the action is held up for six chapters, during which little or nothing is added to the argument. Again it is very significant that Elihu is not mentioned either in the Prologue or Epilogue, or indeed anywhere else in the Book. When we examine the contents of these chapters our impression is confirmed. In the first place, Elihu's literary form is different from that of the rest of the poem. Elsewhere the friends' speeches alternate with those of Job. But Elihu goes straight on for six chapters without a break. There is also a distinctly discernible difference of style; the Elihu speeches are more prolix, more rhetorical, and less powerful than those of either Job or the other friends, though they are not without poetic merit. All modern scholars perhaps without exception, are convinced that these six chapters were added some time later (perhaps as late as the Greek period) by some minor poet who felt that he had something to add to the argument. What he does add, it is not easy to see, but there is a stronger emphasis on suffering as discipline than appears in the rest of the poem. What chiefly concerns the author of the Elihu chapters is not so much that the friends have missed the important arguments, as that they have allowed themselves to be silenced, leaving Job with the last word. However, he strikes a blow for conventional piety, which was offended by the daring words of Job.

Chapter 32

In verse 3 the Hebrew is literally 'and had condemned' Job with no YET. There is a Jewish tradition that the original text was

and had condemned God.

This is very appropriate; Job had condemned God, and the friends by being silent seemed to assent. Elihu is saying in verse 8 that real wisdom comes not from mere age, but from divine inspiration, and such inspiration he claims. Elihu's rash and self-confident words seem to reflect the character of this minor poet. The view which Elihu condemns in verse 13 is the apparent attitude of the three friends: 'We have said our say: now let God convince him, since we cannot.' The sense of verse 14 is: 'Listen to my new arguments, hitherto unconsidered by Job.' In verse 16 we should follow the R.V.:

And shall I wait, because they speak not?

Chapter 33

Elihu's first argument (verse 13) is a return to the basic principle of conventional piety, that you do not ask questions of God. It is therefore a declension from the high personal religion of Job.

Verse 3 is typical of Elihu's self-confident attitude. The meaning of verse 4 is 'I have as good a claim as you to utter wisdom.' But it is balanced by the second half of verse 6, which implies, 'I am not God to terrify you.' We must change the first half of verse 6 to R.V.'s

Behold I am toward God even as thou art.

The second half of verse 13 cannot stand as in the A.V., the
sense is something like:

> Why dost thou strive against him, saying
> He answereth none of my words?

In verses 14 to 18, Elihu is recommending some of the traditional ways of approaching God, but not that personal encounter through faith which Job seeks. He is falling back to
a lower religious level, at which dreams have an important
significance. If we compare Elihu with Eliphaz's experience
in 4.12ff., we must confess that Eliphaz's account is more convincing. He has at any rate an experience of his own to appeal
to, while Elihu is merely referring Job back to traditional ways
of communicating with God. It is a reversion to primitive,
perhaps pagan religion: to this day devotees in India sleep
a night in a temple if they want an answer to prayer. There
is a very striking parallel to this thought in one of the ancient
Greek dramatists, Aeschylus (*Agammemnon*, line 179-183):

> In sleep there drops down upon the heart the grief that
> comes from sin remembered, and wisdom comes even to
> those who desire it not. This irresistible gift surely comes
> from the gods seated on their lofty thrones.

Aeschylus was writing about 450 B.C., and the author of Elihu
certainly wrote after this. The Greek poet has put his finger
on the deepest truth behind the arguments from the varieties
of religious experience drawn by Eliphaz and Elihu, i.e. that
the mind is so constituted that it does tend through the func-
tioning of the subconscious to heal its own wounds. This is
of course the gift of God, who made the mind. Notice that
in verse 14 we should translate 'in one way . . . in another
way' rather than ONCE . . . TWICE. AND SEALETH THEIR
INSTRUCTION in verse 16 is not good sense. The Hebrew is
very doubtful but:

> And dismayeth them with admonitions

is a fair guess.

Verses 19 to 22 describe the sickness which God sends to

discipline men.   In verse 19, THE MULTITUDE OF HIS BONES is wrong.

And with continual strife in his bones (R.V.)

is better sense.   The DESTROYERS in verse 22 refers to the angels of death who were supposed to carry off the souls of the dying. In verse 23 'angel' not MESSENGER should be read.   ONE AMONG A THOUSAND means that:

> Thousands at His bidding speed
> And post o'er land and ocean. . . .

Somehow it is impossible to imagine the keen, profound mind of the author of Job seriously proposing angelic mediation as a solution of the problem of the book.   His UPRIGHTNESS at the end of this verse is not correct:

What is right for him (R.V.)

is better sense.   RANSOM in verse 24 seems to mean the sick man's repentance.   Verse 27 is very obscure in the Hebrew; the following seems a fair reconstruction:

> He (the penitent) singeth before men, and saith,
> I have sinned, and God requited me not.

Verses 31 to 33 make one wonder how the A.V. can say in its chapter-heading: 'Elihu offereth himself instead of God, with sincerity and meekness, to reason with Job.'   There is not much meekness here.

Chapter 34

Elihu's argument is essentially the same as that of the other friends: he argues from the fact of God's almighty power to the conclusion that the working of that power can be followed out by rule of thumb.   We can appreciate why the friends were so much shocked at Job's arguments; if you abandon the traditional account of God's justice, you must choose one of two courses.   You may accept the appalling conclusion that there is no rhyme or reason in the universe at all.   Job skirts this conclusion but never accepts it.   Or you must find a deeper interpretation of God's nature. This task puts far too great a strain on the resources of most men.

Who are the WISE MEN in verse 2? The friends perhaps, or else the author, forgetting that he is supposed to be speaking in the person of Elihu, addresses his readers directly. The first half of verse 6 must be altered to:

> Notwithstanding my right, I am in pain.

SCORNING in verse 7 means: 'scornful talk on sacred subjects'. New and perhaps deeper conceptions are often thus described by the orthodox. For DISPOSED in verse 13 we should read: 'laid upon him' (R.V. margin). The sense seems to be that God rules the world for Himself, not as deputy for someone else, and therefore He cannot be called to account. In verse 14 SET HIS HEART UPON MAN is unsatisfactory. We might read:

> If he were to cause man's spirit to return to Himself.

The doctrine that all life is immediately dependent upon God is certainly an integral part of Christian belief (cf. Acts 17.28), but it is scarcely an answer to Job's problem. With verse 17 compare Genesis 18.25. Translate verse 18 as:

> He saith to a king: Thou art wicked;
> And to princes: Ye are ungodly.

Similarly verse 19 must run:

> He accepteth not the persons of princes . . . etc.

It is very significant that in verse 20 Elihu points to the same evidence to prove his case as Job did to prove his, that is, the sudden changes of fortune in the lives of the great. It goes to show that the question of God's justice cannot be decided simply on the evidence of history, which is after all one of the conclusions of the book. This verse, 20, must be changed to read:

> In a moment they die, and at midnight
> The opulent are smitten and pass away.

In verse 23 Elihu is answering Job's repeated plea for a court

session with God. Elihu says that God needs to make no such
investigation. Moffatt's translation is good here:

God has not to fix sessions, in order to bring men to justice.

WITHOUT NUMBER in verse 24 should be translated 'without
investigation' (as A.V. margin). Change HE STRIKETH THEM
AS WICKED MEN in verse 26 into:

Therefore hath he smitten the wicked. . . .

Verses 29 to 33 must be some of the most obscure verses in
the Bible, not because of their profundity of thought, but because of the imperfect condition of the Hebrew text. A.V.
and R.V., and many an editor, have perseveringly produced
some sort of a meaningful translation, but this can only be
done by treating sentences meaningless in Hebrew as if they
had endings or forms different from what they actually have,
or by obligingly supplying words that are not to be found in
the Hebrew text. A good example is verse 31, the Hebrew
text of which is literally rendered: 'For to God one saith, I
have carried; I will not act corruptly.' Similarly, as the A.V.
margin admits, verse 33 begins with the words: 'From with
thee?' (The question is indicated in the Hebrew.) All we
can safely guess from the passage is that Elihu is suggesting
some course of penitence to Job (the second half of verse 32
is a fair translation in the A.V.) We do not feel that we have
lost very much by the confusion of these verses, but we must
not be betrayed into drawing any lesson or exposition from
them.

Translate the second half of verse 36 as:

Because of his answering like wicked men.

In verse 37 HE CLAPPETH HIS HANDS may mean that Job mocks
at religion.

Chapter 35

A better translation of verse 2 than either A.V. or R.V. is:

Dost thou deem this to be right:
Thou hast said: I am justified before God?

The A.V. margin of verse 3 is right in the second half.

> What profit shall I have by it more than by my sin?

That is, Elihu accuses Job of complaining that righteousness does not pay. This is not fair: Job complains that innocence suffers, which is not the same thing. Elihu, by bringing in the notion of profit and loss reduces the whole discussion to a more superficial level. The fact that Elihu can use the argument he introduces in verse 6 shows how relatively far apart God and men were according to traditional piety. No argument could be more completely overthrown than this one is by the fact of the Cross.

From verse 8 to the end of the chapter we come on another passage where the imperfect nature of the text makes the sense very uncertain. Some think that Elihu is saying that God does not succour the oppressed because they (and among them Job) do not call upon Him in a spirit of true religion. If this is right, it is a new argument in the discussion though not a very illuminating one. But others interpret the passage as Elihu's condemnation of Job because he failed in the past to succour the oppressed. In verse 9 instead of THEY MAKE THE OPPRESSED TO CRY we must follow the R.V. and read:

> men cry out.

Who are the EVIL MEN in verse 12? If we adopt the first of the two interpretations of this passage, it refers to the oppressed themselves (including Job) who are not answered by God because of their pride. If we adopt the second, the evil men are Job and his like who in the past have not answered the cry of the needy. On the whole the first interpretation seems more reasonable. Verse 14 is hopelessly obscure, beyond even intelligent guesswork. The next verse is also obscure, but not desperately so. The A.V. is quite wrong. A small change in the Hebrew gives us:

And now because his anger visiteth not,
And he careth not greatly about transgression. . . .

And so on to verse 16. This means that Job has behaved
so outrageously just because God has been lenient to him or
perhaps to transgressors in general. This is quite a reasonable
sentiment in Elihu's mouth: 'If you really got your
deserts. . . .' It is possibly what Zophar is saying in 11.6,
but see the note there.

Chapter 36
The sense of verse 3 seems to be that Elihu will discuss the
question in general terms, without particular reference to Job.
In verses 8ff. Elihu explains away all apparent exceptions to
the prosperity of the righteous as examples of disciplinary
suffering. He elaborates this idea and emphasizes that God
always explains to those thus disciplined the meaning of their
sufferings. HEAP UP WRATH in verse 13 means 'cherish resent-
ment' at their sufferings without trying to understand them.
In verse 14 UNCLEAN is apparently a reference to the male
temple-prostitutes who had been, in the past at least, a feature
of Semitic religion. Their lives were proverbially short.
Scholars' guesses as to the meaning of verse 16 are so divergent
that it is best to abandon any attempt to translate it. Verse 18
is also very difficult, but Moffatt seems to have produced the
best attempt:

Let not his chastening make you rage at him,
Let not the cost of discipline deter you.

'The cost of discipline' is the sufferings which are to save him
from the effects of his sin. The sense of verse 19 is almost
beyond recovery; it may be a suggestion that all Job's former
wealth was no use to him without the discipline of suffering.
One editor remarks of verse 20: 'The Hebrew is nonsense
and the suggested emendations unsatisfactory.' We may leave
it at that.

From verse 24 to the end of chapter 37 the text becomes less uncertain. Elihu passes from his not very original arguments to a fine panegyric of the divine power as displayed in the operations of the weather. The first part of verse 26 is a famous tag. It is better translated:

> Behold God is great, and we know not how great.

It has often been quoted in support of a 'reverent agnosticism', which is the very last thing that the author of these chapters would have approved. The A.V. of verse 27 has somehow lost the reference to the sea which is in the original Hebrew. We should translate:

> For he draweth up drops from the sea.

THE NOISE OF HIS TABERNACLES in verse 29 means the sound of the thunder reverberating in the sky, which was thought of as God's tent. In verse 30 HE COVERETH THE BOTTOM OF THE SEA is poor sense. We should probably read:

> He covereth the tops of the mountains.

The A.V. of verse 32 is wrong; the R.V. is probably nearer the original

> He covereth his hands with the lightning,
> And giveth it a charge that it strike the mark.

God is apparently depicted as dwelling in light (cf. I Timothy 6.16) and detaching a certain portion of it to strike as lightning. Verse 33 is not very certain; the CATTLE seems a little incongruous. Here is a fair guess:

> The thunder declareth his indignation,
> And the storm proclaimeth his anger.

Chapter 37

In verse 1 IS MOVED is too mild a translation: 'leapeth' is

better. THEM in verse 4 seems to refer to the flashes of lightning. Verse 6 should probably run:

> He saith to the snow, Fall thou on the earth,
> To the monsoon and the rain, Drop down.

The sense of verse 7 is that in winter God makes work in the fields impossible. Instead of SOUTH and NORTH in verse 9, we should read: 'chambers' and 'storehouses' respectively. The author of Elihu shares the Hebrew belief that wind, rain, snow, etc., were brought by God from special storehouses where He kept them when not in use, cf. Ps. 135.7; Job 38.22. We should translate verses 11 and 12 as:

> He ladeth the cloud with moisture,
> And the cloud scattereth his light.
> And he maketh them go round about,
> His guidance maketh them change.

OR FOR HIS LAND, the literal translation of the Hebrew in verse 13, is nonsense in this context. Here is another rendering:

> Whether for a rod or for a curse,
> Or for mercy, that he causeth it to find its mark.

The cloud may bring either lightning to destroy or rain to bless. In verse 16 THE BALANCINGS OF THE CLOUDS means the marvellous way in which these heavy rain-laden clouds seem to be poised in the air.

Having dealt with other weather conditions, Elihu now speaks of the hot, oppressive day when no cloud is to be seen. Leave out the AND in the second half of verse 18, and the sense becomes clear. Verse 19 is ironical. The sense of verse 20 seems to be: 'What does it matter to God whether I speak? Anyone who dared to argue with Him would be consumed with awe.' A better translation of verse 21 seems to be:

> And now the light cannot be seen;
> It is obscured by the clouds.

It is a description of a cloudy day. Verse 23 emphasizes the inscrutability of God, a favourite theme with the friends, though not very consistent in Elihu's mouth, seeing he claims to have the full explanation of God's way.

So ends the Elihu Interpolation. We must try to imagine that we pass straight from the end of chapter 31 to the beginning of chapter 38, if we are to envisage the Book as its author intended it to be.

V

GOD'S APPEARANCE AND JOB'S SUBMISSION

Chapter 38, verse 1, to Chapter 42, verse 6

Chapter 38 **God Answers Job**

God's answer is only satisfying to Job if his main desire was for a personal encounter with God rather than simply for an explanation of the problem of his sufferings. God now breaks His silence, of which Job had complained (e.g. 9.11), but He does not lay aside His glory. He speaks out of the whirlwind, not as man to man as Job asked. Before the coming of Christ it was impossible for a Jew to represent the Almighty Jehovah as coming down and speaking as man with men. Hence this appearance of God is one of the finest answers which the O.T. provides to the desire of man for personal communion. The next two chapters contain some magnificent poetry describing God's majesty in the glorious works of nature.

The WHIRLWIND in verse 1 was the traditional accompaniment of God's appearances; cf. Psalm 18.9 and 10; I Kings 19.11; Ezekiel 1.4. God appears in answer to Job's repeated challenge, but He does not provide any answer to Job's questions. He does not condemn Job as guilty of the charges which the friends have speculatively laid against him. Instead He overpowers Job by His majesty as manifested first in natural phenomena, and then in the animal creation. SONS OF GOD in verse 7 means the stars, which in Semitic mythology were often thought of as angelic beings. The sea was identified with Tiamat the chaos-monster (See Introduction, p. 12); so

the reference in verse 8 is to the process of creation whereby
the monster was tamed, and its activity limited by the bounds
of the dry land.   In verse 9 CLOUDS AND DARKNESS are represented as the extreme limit of the ocean.   A.V. is astray in
verse 10;

> and prescribed for it my decree

(A.V. margin and R.V.) is better than AND BRAKE UP FOR IT
MY DECREED PLACE.

The first line of verse 11 was used by Charles Stewart
Parnell in a famous speech, and is carved on his monument
in O'Connell St., Dublin.   He said that no man had a right to
say this: ' to the march of a nation.'   The author of Job would
have emphatically maintained that *God* had.   The figure in
verse 13 is curious: the dawn, casting light over the earth, is
like one who shakes a coverlet from a bed, shaking off dust.
In the same way the wicked, whose deeds are done in darkness, are shown up and frustrated by the coming of the light.
Verse 14 continues the reference to dawn; the earth is cast into
high relief like clay stamped with a seal.   The second half
must be emended to:

> And (the earth) is dyed like a garment.

The meaning of verse 15 is that, since the light of the wicked
is darkness, when darkness goes their opportunity for doing
mischief goes also.   Translate the HIGH ARM as ' the uplifted
arm '.   SEARCH in verse 16 means ' recesses '.   The sense of
verse 20 is: ' Are you able to conduct the daylight to its rest-
ing place when night comes? '   The DAY of verse 23 seems
to mean the time for God's using His natural resources to
punish the wicked.   As we shall see later, God appears to be
saying that He does govern the world, but according to His
own methods.   We must follow the R.V. in the second half of
verse 24:

> ' Or the east wind scattered upon the earth? '

In verses 25 to 27 another marvel of God's activity is de-

scribed, the apparent purposelessness of some of His actions.
He wastes good rain on the desert. It is all part of His inscrutability. In Matthew 5.45 a different conclusion is drawn
from a similar phenomenon. The generosity of God is shown
in His giving rain to those who do not deserve it. The detailed
interpretation of verses 31 to 32 is uncertain, since we know
so little about Hebrew astronomy. Modern editors prefer to
translate verse 31 (following R.V.) as:

> Canst thou bind the cluster of the Pleiades,
> Or loose the bond of Orion?

The one line challenges Job to do something that God has
done, the other to undo something that God has done.
(See page 12 for the Hebrew belief about Orion.) Scholars
have been unable to determine which constellation or planet
MAZZAROTH indicates. The second half of verse 33 may refer
simply to the fact that the earth is dependent on the weather,
and hence could be described as ' under the dominion of the
heavens '. But it may refer to astrology, the belief that human
destinies are influenced by the movements of the stars.
Astrology in the time of the author of Job was a respectable
science, as it still is to-day in Hindu India, and was in the
Middle Ages in Europe. In fact our author's belief may be
very well compared with that of the orthodox astrologers of
medieval times. They, like him, never for a moment doubted
that the dominion exercised by the stars is completely subject
to God's authority.

Instead of INWARD PARTS and HEART in verse 36, we should
probably translate ' clouds ' and ' cloud-wrack ' respectively.
In that case WISDOM and UNDERSTANDING refer to the complicated laws governing the operations of the clouds. The
chapter should really end with verse 38, for in the next verse
we turn from heavenly phenomena to marvels of the animal
creation, a theme which continues till the end of chapter 39.
As we have noticed before, much of the force of God's argument seems to lie in its appeal to the unaccountability of God.
In verse 40 God is described as doing something that Job

would never think of doing, even if he could. He provides food for the lions, man's natural foes. With verse 41, compare Psalm 147.9; Matthew 6.26.

Chapter 39

In this chapter we begin by considering the beasts who are least amenable to man. But God knows them. We can detect in this a desire to correct the outlook of Job and his friends, who tended to judge all God's activities too much by the standard of man's needs. There is a certain resemblance to our Lord's teaching here: He describes the care of God for the natural creation, quite apart from its utility or uselessness to man: cf. Matthew 10.29.

THEIR SORROWS in verse 3 should probably be 'their young'. GOOD LIKING in verse 4 means simply 'good health'. WITH CORN in the same verse is a mistranslation: 'in the open field' of the R.V. is correct. The meaning is that they manage their lives without any reference to man. Not MULTITUDE in verse 7, but 'tumult' or 'noise' (R.V.). UNICORN in verse 9 is a picturesque translation, but 'wild-ox' (R.V.) is better. It seems to be the aurochs, which was found in the Jordan valley at least as late as 600 B.C. The first part of verse 10 should probably run:

> Dost thou bind him to the furrow with cords?

Except that there is a reference to the ostrich in verse 13, the sense is quite uncertain. PEACOCK of the A.V. is certainly wrong. The second half of verse 16 is better translated:

> That her labour may be in vain, she hath no care.

Verse 17 is probably a later insertion; God speaks in the first person throughout the rest of the chapter. LIFTETH UP HERSELF ON HIGH in verse 18 represents a word in Hebrew which is unknown to scholars:

> spurreth herself on with her short wings

is a better guess. The ostrich was proverbial both for her cruelty (cf. Lamentations 4.3) and her stupidity. Both these

THE BOOK OF JOB 39.18-24

qualities are underlined here. This is in line with the whole of
God's speech, which emphasizes how unlike these creatures are
to man. The ostrich behaves in this unreasonable manner, and
yet God made her so. This verse also suggests that with all
her stupidity she can outstrip man's best efforts at speed. It is
in this sense that we must understand the A.V. chapter head-
ing: 'The Lord answereth Job and convinceth him of ignor-
ance and imbecility.' 'Imbecility' in the seventeenth century
meant powerlessness and not mental weakness.

We turn in verse 19 to the war horse, tamed and trained by
man, but not on that account to be thought of as inferior to
man. The horse was for the Hebrews of this period what the
elephant became later on, and what the tank is for us to-day—
a really decisive weapon in war. When Ahab was able in
853 B.C. to supply two thousand chariots to the coalition that
successfully resisted the Assyrians at Karkar, it was a sign
that Israel was at a great pitch of power. In very early days
they had no horses, and could only hope to conquer in a battle
of the plains when helped by weather-conditions, as they did
for example against Sisera, in Judges 5. So the war horse is a
symbol of great power which man can use but not create.
CLOTHED HIS NECK WITH THUNDER is unfortunately incorrect,
though Dryden has immortalized the phrase:

> Clothed his neck with strength

is probably a better translation. Verse 20 should run, as in
R.V.

> Hast thou made him to leap as a locust?
> The glory of his snorting is terrible.

For THE QUIVER RATTLETH in verse 23 a better reading is:

> the bow twangeth.

The trumpet seems to have crept into verse 24 from the next
verse. It is better to follow Moffatt's vivid rendering:

> But on he charges in wild rage,
> Straight ahead, never swerving.

HA HA in the English of verse 25 represents a far more onoma-
topœic sound in the Hebrew, which really reproduces much
more closely the snort of a horse. In verses 28 to 30 we meet
again the emphasis on the activity of God's creatures in which
puny man can have no part, with the same hint that they
behave in a way unnatural to man (for example in their
ferocity), and yet God has ordained them to be so.

Chapter 40, verses 1 and 2, and 6 to 14 **God's Speech Con-
cluded**

Scholars have often pointed out the unsatisfactory way in
which Job's capitulation appears at verse 3 in chapter 40.
God apparently takes no notice of it, but continues His
majestic reply to Job. It does seem very likely that Job's reply
in 40.3-5 and 42.2-6 are really two parts of the same speech that
have somehow got separated. We therefore print them together
as a single speech after our commentary on God's reply.

Verse 1 will thus be the addition of a later editor writing
after the disintegration had taken place; cf. 29.1. Verse 6
must also be put in this category. In verse 8 God accuses Job
of measuring His actions by the yardstick of his own limited
knowledge. If man asserts his own righteousness in the way
that Job did, he inevitably denies God's righteousness. In
verses 10 to 14 God seems to be saying to Job: 'You have
condemned me for not conducting the government of the world
on the principle of rewards for the pious and punishments for
the wicked. But you have not yourself the power to conduct
it on this principle, so you have no right to condemn me for
not doing so.' This is indeed a condemnation of Job's attitude,
but far more of the friends' arguments. They never doubted
for a moment that the government of the world is conducted
on just these simple principles. Job challenges this assumption, and God tacitly agrees that Job has fact on his side. For
IN SECRET, verse 13, we should probably read with the R.V.:

in the hidden place.

i.e. She'ol. Verse 14 forms quite a suitable ending to God's

speech: the RIGHT HAND must refer primarily to Job's uprightness of which he was so confident.

Chapter 40, verses 3 to 5, and Chapter 42, verses 2 to 6   **Job's
Submission**
   Then Job answered the Lord and said:

> Behold I am vile; what shall I answer thee?
>   I will lay mine hand upon my mouth.
> Once have I spoken; but I will not answer:
>   Yea twice; but I will proceed no further.
> I know that thou canst do everything.
>   And that no purpose of thine can be restrained.
> Therefore have I uttered things that I should not;
>   Things too wonderful for me that I knew not.
> I have heard of thee by the hearing of the ear:
>   But now mine eye seeth thee.
> Wherefore I repudiate my words,
>   And repent in dust and ashes.

In 40.5 ONCE . . . TWICE only means 'a number of times'.
Chapter 42.1 must be understood as an editor's insertion after
the original text had become dislocated. Instead of NO
THOUGHT CAN BE WITHOLDEN FROM THEE in 42.2 we should
follow the R.V. and read:

> No purpose of thine can be restrained.

It seems that what Job is repudiating in these verses is his
more or less explicit questioning of God's ability or will to
govern the world rightly. He still fails to understand how
God does it, but is now willing to leave it in God's hands
as he was not before. In the first sentence of 42.3 and
the whole of verse 4 we have quotations from God's speech
in 38.2 and 3. They do not fit very smoothly into either
the thought or the verse structure of the poem. It is likely
that:

WHO IS HE THAT HIDETH COUNSEL WITHOUT KNOWLEDGE?
HEAR I BESEECH THEE, AND I WILL SPEAK
I WILL DEMAND OF THEE, AND DECLARE THOU UNTO ME

were originally marginal comments written in by a scribe who wished to reinforce the lesson of Job's repentance. Subsequent copyists incorporated them into the text. The contrast in 42.5 is between orthodox tradition (i.e. what Job had heard of God) and personal experience and conviction (i.e. what Job was now seeing for himself). This seeing for himself comes very near to what the N.T. calls faith. In 42.6, as the A.V. admits, MYSELF is not to be found in the Hebrew; it is therefore probably better to take the meaning as:

I repudiate (my words).

Third Interpolation

Chapter 40, verse 15, to Chapter 41, verse 34 **The Hippopotamus and the Crocodile**

Chapter 40, verses 15 to 24 **The Hippopotamus**

The contents and style of these two descriptions of animals make it fairly plain that they did not originally belong to the speech of God in chapters 38 and 39, or indeed to the poem itself. They are not punctuated with the frequent, scornful questions that interrupt God's speech, neither do they emphasize the irrational, or at least inhuman characteristics of the animals that we observed previously. The author of these descriptions is more interested in the unusual size and strength of the two animals. The words BEHEMOTH and LEVIATHAN are only Hebrew words written out in English letters. Most modern editors agree that their respective meanings are 'hippopotamus' and 'crocodile'. The A.V. margin suggests 'elephant' for behemoth, but the description fits the hippopotamus better.

In verse 15 WITH THEE means 'he is my creature as well as you'. The CEDAR in verse 17 usually signifies strength and length. Our author must have been misinformed about the hippopotamus' tail. Translate the second sentence in the verse as:

The sinews of his thighs are knit together (R.V.)

We must also follow the R.V. in verse 18:

> His bones are as tubes of brass;
> His limbs are like bars of iron.

The hyperbolical description in the first half of verse 19 seems only to mean that he is among the greatest of God's creatures. Translate the second half as:

> Let him that made him make his sword to approach unto him.

i.e. only God can conquer him. The MOUNTAINS in verse 20 are probably the low hills surrounding the Nile. Both these animals belonged to Egypt, not Palestine, at least in historical times. It seems likely that some Hebrew poet had visited Egypt and wanted to record its marvels in verse. Perhaps he had no thought that his poem would come to form part of the Book of Job. WHERE ALL THE BEASTS OF THE FIELD PLAY seems to indicate the harmlessness of the hippopotamus. Translate verses 23 and 24 as the R.V.:

> Behold, if a river overflow, he trembleth not:
> He is confident, though Jordan swell even to his mouth.
> Shall any take him when he is on the watch,
> Or pierce through his nose with a snare?

Chapter 41 The Crocodile

Leviathan is, as we saw above, in all probability the crocodile, though there may be some comparison between it and the mythological chaos-monster. The first eight verses of this chapter, with their interrogative form, seem rather different in tone from the rest, but it is difficult to attribute them to the author of Job.

Follow the R.V. in the second half of verse 1:

> Or press down his tongue with a cord?

In verse 6 the COMPANIONS means 'the bands of fishermen'; cf. Luke 5.7. The sense of verse 8 is that the lightest touch

will bring dire retribution. Verse 9 appears to be referring
to the man who is rash enough to lay his hand on the crocodile.
We should probably change the first half of verse 10 to:

> Is he not fierce if one rouse him up?

Who is ME in verse 11? Is it God? Probably not, but the
crocodile represented as speaking. We must translate:

> Who ever confronted me and was safe?

St. Paul, assuming that the sentence is spoken by God, quotes
it in Romans 11.35. The fact of its not being suited to its
context would not disturb St. Paul. He uses it to illustrate his
own deep theme that we cannot put God in our debt. The
same theme is certainly found in the Book of Job, but is
definitely out of place here. Verse 13 could mean 'his two
rows of teeth', but most editors alter the Hebrew to read:

> his double coat of mail

Strange as it may seem, the crocodile does sneeze a lot, as
described in verse 18. In Egyptian hieroglyphics the dawn is
indicated by the crocodile's eyes, which appear red when look-
ing up from just under the surface of the water. The SPARKS
OF FIRE in verses 19 and 21 must not be taken literally. It
refers to the sparkling of the drops of water which he spouts
up into the air. The second half of verse 22 must be translated as in the R.V.:

> Terror danceth before him,

a fine phrase. So also in the second half of verse 25 we must
follow the R.V.:

> His underparts are like sharp potsherds:
> He spreadeth as it were a threshing wain upon the mire.

DEEP and SEA in verses 31 and 32 refer to the Nile; cf. Isaiah
19.5 and Nahum 3.8, where rivers are described in terms of
the sea. The POT OF OINTMENT is the pan in which the per-

fume is manufactured. It boils and froths in the process. A slight alteration in verse 34 gives the much better translation:

All high things fear him.

THE CHILDREN OF PRIDE are the greater beasts.

From the literary point of view these detailed descriptions of hippopotamus and crocodile are remarkable as showing an interest in the natural creation unusual in the O.T. But what connection have they with the message of the Book of Job, the revelation of God's purpose in the O.T., or the Christian religion? Very little indeed. From a religious point of view, they are the wrappings in which the treasure is enclosed. They are chiefly valuable as a witness that when God speaks through men He does not destroy their human nature. He guarantees them from neither fallibility nor irrelevance. Our task as Christians is first and foremost to recognize this irrelevant material for what it is, and not to try to find hidden meanings or deep secrets in it.

THE EPILOGUE
Chapter 42, verse 7 to end

We now return to the prose narrative, and find ourselves again in the simple, fairy-tale atmosphere of the patriarchal age. Job receives entire restitution for what he has lost, the friends are rebuked, and everyone lives happily ever afterwards. We are not to imagine that our author intends to convey more by the Epilogue than Job's restoration after his repentance. The details of the legend only combine to emphasize this one point and are of no particular significance in themselves. If one can imagine a play in which the theme of *King Lear* was set against the kind of background of *The Tempest*, with its fairy-tale 'they all lived happily ever after' ending, this will give some idea of the difference in atmosphere.

As we read verse 7, we cannot help feeling that the friends receive a rebuke, and Job a commendation, out of all proportion to what they actually said in the poem. One suggestion which would explain this is that in the original legend the friends, like Job's wife, incited him to rebellion, and he met them with answers of steadfast piety. Our author has reversed the rôles. The SEVEN BULLOCKS AND SEVEN RAMS in verse 8 simply imply a very large sacrifice, reminiscent of Balak's in Numbers 23.29. Probably the Prologue and Epilogue are intended to recall some such legendary age. We need not imagine that there are any deep lessons about intercessory prayers to be drawn from this verse. Instead of LEST I DEAL WITH YOU AFTER YOUR FOLLY we should read:

> lest I deal with you in an unseemly way.

i.e. 'lest I punish you'. In verse 9 Elihu is not mentioned, a strong argument against the Elihu passages having been a part of the original poem. Notice that in verse 10ff. there is no mention of the healing of the disease from which Job is described as suffering. Did the poet perhaps set out with the legendary story, in which Job suffers from the disease, and did his own experience of social degradation break in and eclipse the other theme? Job's social downfall seems to be described from personal experience. Some readers of Job have expressed disappointment that after a poem that deals with such high spiritual problems, the restoration should be expressed in purely material terms. But in fact the author has chosen to express the restoration in terms of the legend, and this is the language of legend. Cinderella must marry the prince and live happily ever afterward. The PIECE OF MONEY in verse 11 is a 'qesitah', a coin of unknown value that seems to belong to the patriarchal age: cf. Joshua 24.32. The EAR-RING of the A.V. goes a little beyond the evidence. It may have been a ring for the finger, or even for the nose; cf. Genesis 24.47, where the R.V. reads 'and I put the ring upon her nose.' In India to-day the nose-ring is still considered a normal ornament for a woman, and, in the villages, even for a man. The number of the animals in verse 12 is exactly double what we met with in the Prologue. Why the numbers SEVEN and THREE for sons and daughters in verse 13? Any sensible man in the East to this day wants to have more sons than daughters; seven and three are both sacred numbers. The daughters also have fairy-tale names: JEMIMA is 'dove', KEZIAH is 'cassia', a fragant perfume; KEREN-HAPPUCH is 'box of antimony', a cosmetic. We might paraphrase by 'Swansdown', 'Lavender', and 'Mascara'. And of course, as we learn in verse 15, they were more beautiful than any other maidens in the land. Job's extreme age of which we are told in verse 16 is but another witness to the fact that, whereas in the poem he is a living man, wrestling with the deepest problems of life, in the Epilogue he is a legendary prince, doing all the things that a patriarch was supposed to do.

POSTSCRIPT

It is seventeen years since this commentary was first published. During the interval, we have been able to realize both how rash and how necessary was the enterprise of writing a popular commentary on the Book of Job. It was rash because it was attempting to express in a small book the essence of a vast amount of scholarly research, written by scholars in three languages, research which is continuing unabated, and which every few years shows itself in the production of huge commentaries on the Book running into hundreds of pages. But the enterprise was also apparently necessary, because this commentary has gone on selling through the years. There must be many people who want to explore the Book of Job, who have neither the time nor the expertise to read the bigger commentaries.

It cannot be said that during these seventeen years scholarly opinion on the Book has undergone any great revolutionary change. It is still fair to say that the majority of scholars regard both the Wisdom chapter (28) and the Elihu speeches as later additions, not part of the original poem. Perhaps there has been a tendency to move away from the problem of suffering as the central theme, and to suggest that the theme may be a still more existential one, the mystery of life, or the mystery of God Himself, a tendency which rather confirms the approach adopted in our commentary. Thus A. Weiser writes: 'The Book of Job is not a didactic poem, but a book about life (*ein Lebensbuch*)'. It is also fair to say that scholarly opinion by and large still supports a post-exilic date for the final form of the Book, and that the earlier suggestions of an Egyptian or Edomite origin for the author are now very widely rejected in favour of a Palestinian origin.

More Babylonian and Egyptian material which offers some sort of a parallel to the story of Job has turned up or been brought forward in evidence. To question the ways of God or the gods, to conclude that man can really know nothing about providence, this sort of speculation had been going on for a long time in the Middle East. This helps to determine the class of literature into which the Book of Job may be said to fall, but it still offers no parallel at all to what the Book of Job actually says about these subjects. We should add that, contrary to what we say on p. 35 of our commentary, some fragments of the Book of Job in Hebrew have now turned up among the Qumran finds.

Even more interesting, some fragments of a Targum on Job have been found. A Targum is an Aramaic paraphrase on Scripture provided for those Jews who heard the Scriptures read in Hebrew in the synagogue but who could not understand biblical Hebrew. This find is interesting because it shows that a Targum on Job had already been written down by Paul's day. Now Paul, as we pointed out, does occasionally quote Job. But we omitted one quotation which, just because of its abstruseness, may have had great significance for Paul. In Romans 11.35 Paul quotes Job 41.11 in the following form:

Or who hath first given unto him, and it shall be recompensed unto him again?

In fact if you look up Job 41.11 you will find a very different translation:

Who hath prevented me that I should repay him?
Whatsoever is under the whole heaven is mine.

Paul has in fact followed a Greek translation which rendered the Hebrew quite differently to the way the A.V. translators rendered it. But there is some evidence that Paul's translation, or something like it, was known to the Jewish scholars of his day. The significance of Paul's translation is that it shows the influence of the Targum, and the Targum tradition had probably already by Paul's day got to work on the original text so as to import into it metaphysical and theological overtones which were certainly not in the mind of the author. Thus what was originally a description of the fearsome appearance of the crocodile has been transformed into an indirect reference to the pre-existent Wisdom of God, who was his agent in creation. It would be far too complicated to produce here the evidence to justify this conclusion; but it means that, as far as Paul at least is concerned, we must add one more aspect of the Book of Job. In it he thought he could trace occasional reference to the pre-existent Wisdom of God which he identified with the Son.

In fairness to the Jewish scholars who lived in Paul's day and after it, we should add that in many ways the real significance of the Book was better appreciated by them than it was by many early Christians. Some of the Rabbis were deeply offended by Job's rash accusations against God: Dust, they say, should be put in his mouth for his blasphemous suggestions. Others were of the opinion that the blasphemous accusations should be attributed to Satan and not to Job. Still others draw a very interesting parallel between Job and Abraham: both, they point out, were tempted by God's permission (see Genesis 22, the sacrifice of Isaac). One Rabbi is actually recorded as having made the bold suggestion that Job never lived; the whole tale was perhaps a parable. But his suggestion did not commend itself to many of his colleagues. In our review of religious opinion about the Book of Job, we should therefore distinguish the Rabbis as having recorded some independent and penetrating insights.

Finally, we should mention one or two books in English published since we wrote. Most important of all is E. Dhorme's great commentary, originally published in French in 1926, which has in 1967 been translated and published in English with a brief foreword by H. H. Rowley. This has been acclaimed as the best commentary ever to be written on Job. Anyone who wishes to study the book in detail must consult it. A small book was published by Edgar Jones in 1966 with the SCM Press, called *The Triumph of Job,* which has a useful discussion of the theme of the Book; he sums up the theme thus: 'a religion without strings is gloriously possible'. More weighty is Dr Norman Snaith's book, published in 1968 in *Studies in Biblical Theology* (second series) by the SCM Press: *The Book of Job: Its origin and purpose.* This is not a full commentary on the text, but an exposition, backed by great linguistic and literary knowledge, of a view that sees the Book as a unity. According to Dr Snaith, there is only one author. He first told the legend afresh, inserting into it his original poem, a single speech by Job and a reply by the High God. At later dates, on further reflection, the same author added first the speeches of the friends and then in old age the Elihu speeches—the old man in a burst of longing for lost youth imagines the angel of death bringing a sudden reprieve to the righteous. It is too soon to judge how other Old Testament scholars react to Dr Snaith's approach. His conclusions have a lot in common with those of a Rabbi of today, Rabbi Gordis, but among Christian critical commentators, he stands alone.

Since 1953 three important new English translations of the Old Testament have appeared, the Revised Standard Version, the Jerusalem Bible, and the New English Bible. Any one of these is, as a translation, very much more accurate than the Authorized Version. Nobody today should be content to read the Book of Job in the Authorized Version only. We would specially recommend either of the last two new versions.

Hull, May 1970   Anthony and Miriam Hanson